MICKEY ROGERS
JOANNE TAYLORE-KNOWLES
STEVE TAYLORE-KNOWLES

SPEAK YOUR MIND

STUDENT'S BOOK
+ access to Student's App and Digital Workbook

3A

macmillan education

SCOPE & SEQUENCE

	Outcomes	Vocabulary	Grammar	Speaking
Unit 1 Incredible Lives pp. 7–15	• Discuss possible devices that could help disabled people • Ask and answer questions about your achievements • Describe survival situations	• Technology and disability • Noun suffixes • Character adjectives	• Stative and dynamic verbs • Expressing ability Grammar Reference pp 142–143	• Describe a device to help disabled people • Talk about personal achievements • Talk about survival situation
	Language and Life—Decision Making: Manage a Survival Situation			
Unit 2 The Animal Connection pp. 17–25	• Talk about which are the most intelligent animals • Discuss possible jobs with animals • Make arguments for and against people owning exotic pets	• Animal intelligence • Careers with animals • Animals	• Tag questions • Articles Grammar Reference pp 143–144	• Discuss which animals are most intelligent • Talk about working with animals • Argue for and against keeping wild animals
	Language and Life—Problem Solving: Find Solutions to Help Stray Animals			
Unit 3 Think About It pp. 27–35	• Ask and answer questions about confirmation bias • Discuss the importance of expert systems in your future career • Compare different creative uses for things	• Confirmation bias • Word formation • Phrasal verbs	• Future time clauses (*after*, *as soon as*, *before*, *until*, *when*) • Present perfect progressive Grammar Reference pp 145–146	• Discuss confirmation bias • Talk about expert systems • Compare different objects
	Language and Life—Design Thinking: Design an App			
Unit 4 Beyond Words pp. 37–45	• Present a subject you know • Ask questions and assess someone's body language • Decide on the best means of communication for different situations	• Communication • Ways to communicate • Emojis	• Infinitives with *to* • Separable and non-separable phrasal verbs Grammar Reference pp 146–147	• Give a presentation • Make statements about yourself • Discuss ways to communicate
	Language and Life—Reason Effectively: Discuss Ideas to Improve Communication Problems			
Unit 5 One Planet pp. 47–55	• Discuss global warming problems • Talk about solutions • Brainstorm products	• Climate change • Taking action • Materials and products	• Review of conditionals • Present and future hopes and wishes Grammar Reference pp 148–149	• Discuss global warming • Discuss environmental solutions • Discuss if measures are practical
	Language and Life—Global Competence: Explain and Discuss Ideas about Environmental Issues			
Unit 6 Moments in Time pp. 57–65	• Compare different generational use of technology • Share your opinions about inventions • Brainstorm quiz questions about people in history	• Change • *–ed* and *–ing* adjectives • Adjective suffixes	• Past perfect • Defining relative clauses Grammar Reference pp 149–150	• Compare lists • Discuss an opinion poll • Create a quiz
	Language and Life—Decision Making: Choose a New UNESCO Site			

Confident Communicator	Pronunciation	Listening/Reading	Thinking Skills	Writing
Start Talking • Start a discussion *Repair It* • Express lack of understanding *Keep Talking* • Justify choices	• Word stress with *–ity*	Read an article about technology and disability • Skill—Predict information Listen to part of a lecture about amazing abilities • Skill—Recognize signposts Listen to a podcast about Juliane Koepcke • Skill—Listen for specific information	• Apply • Evaluate • Analyze	Write a blog post about a survival situation
Unit Review p. 16 **Study Skills**—Effective Time Management				
Keep Talking • Invite agreement *Start Talking* • Hypotheticals *Keep Talking* • Disagree politely	• *The*	Read a blog post about animal intelligence • Skill—Understand examples Listen to a careers talk • Skill—Use key information to predict content Listen to a zoo's presentation • Skill—Listen for key words	• Recall • Analyze • Evaluate	Write an opinion post
Unit Review p. 26 **Follow a Pro**—A Wildlife Photographer ▶ Marine Biologist				
Keep Talking • Give yourself time to think *Start Talking* • Start talking *Keep Talking* • Further suggestions	• say, says, said	Read an article about confirmation bias • Skill—Identify the topic Listen to a radio call-in show about AI • Skill—Listen for attitude Listen to a talk about being creative • Skill—Listen for main ideas	• Analyze • Evaluate • Apply	Write an informal email about being productive
Unit Review p. 36 **Study Skills**—Making a Presentation or Giving a Talk				
Keep Talking • Speak to a group *Keep Talking* • Provide more information *Keep Talking* • Make meaning clearer	• Electronic communication	Read an article about communication • Skill—Read for gist Listen to a podcast • Skill—Listen for specific information Listen to a lecture about communication technology • Skill—Listen for the order of events	• Evaluate • Apply • Predict	Write an informal text message as a formal email
Unit Review p. 46 **Follow a Pro**—A PR Professional ▶ Translator/Interpreter				
Start Talking • Speak for a group *Keep Talking* • Talk about problems and solutions *Keep Talking* • Comment on ideas	• Word stress in verb phrases	Read an online article about climate change • Skill— Identify explanations, definitions, and examples Listen to a radio show about environmental problems • Skill—Listen for main ideas Listen to a class discussion about environmental solutions • Skill—Listen for details	• Summarize • Analyze • Categorize	Write an essay about environmental projects
Unit Review p. 56 **Study Skills**—Improving Reading Speed				
Keep Talking • Circumlocution *Keep Talking* • Interrupting politely *Keep Talking* • Express interest and surprise	• Stress in multisyllable adjectives	Read an article about technological changes • Skill—Scan Listen to some interviews about inventions • Skill—Listen for supporting details Listen to a podcast about a famous person • Skill—Listen for numerical information	• Predict • Evaluate • Question	Write a short biographical essay
Unit Review p. 66 **Follow a Pro**—An Archeologist ▶ Mechanical Engineer				

Grammar Quiz: What Do You Already Know?

A Complete the paragraph with the simple past, past progressive, or present perfect form of the verbs in parentheses.

Colombian teen Yadis Xiomara Chocó Mina has a clear goal: to help others. She **1** ______________ (work) to improve the lives of young girls since she was nine years old. She **2** ______________ (work) with a group called Plan International Colombia when she first **3** ______________ (start) to mentor young girls in her community. Since then, she **4** ______________ (not stop). A few years ago, while she **5** ______________ (visit) Spain, she **6** ______________ (become) mayor of Madrid for a day as part of International Day of the Girl. Yadis has big plans: someday she wants to be Colombia's minister of education.

B Complete the email message with the correct quantifiers from the box.

a few	a little	a lot of	any	enough	too much

New Message

Hi Anna,

I'm home preparing for Ricardo's graduation party. I've finished most of the preparations, but I could use **1** ______________ help. There are going to be **2** ______________ people here—I think about 45 of his friends are coming. We have 40 chairs, but it's not **3** ______________. Can you bring **4** ______________ chairs—maybe three or four? I know we have **5** ______________ food, so there will be leftovers for the guests to take home. So, please don't bring **6** ______________ more food. There is nowhere to put it!

See you soon,
Bev

C Choose the correct option.

1. **Can** / **Would** you like to join us?
2. I'm sure Oscar **will** / **may** be here.
3. **Will** / **May** I put my jacket here?
4. **Could** / **May** you please take a seat?
5. Lena **might** / **would** be late for the wedding.
6. They probably **won't** / **might not** be there.

D Complete the sentences with the correct form of the verb in parentheses.

1. If you ______________ (eat) a lot of sugar, you gain weight.
2. If I ______________ (have) more time, I would exercise more.
3. You will enjoy these brain puzzles if you ______________ (try) them.
4. If I ______________ (get) tired at the library, I usually take a short nap.
5. I probably ______________ (not go) to the hospital if I had a bad cold.
6. You ______________ (not feel) better if you don't take this medicine.

E Find one error in each sentence. Then rewrite the sentences correctly.

1. Maggie has belonged to a gym since 15 years.
   ____
2. Rafael hasn't graduated from high school already.
   ____
3. A lot cans and plastic are recycled these days.
   ____
4. People use to buy a lot of music CDs in the 1990s.
   ____
5. Jae is the more adventurous person in my family.
   ____
6. Students need to introduce themself in class.
   ____

Go to the Grammar Review on pages 140–141.

UNIT 1 Incredible Lives

WHAT DO YOU ALREADY KNOW?

1 Think about your family: what characteristics do you share with them and which are unique to you? Write the words.

2 **IN PAIRS** Share and compare your ideas. If possible, add more words about yourself or your partner.

Shared characteristics

Unique characteristics

DISCUSS & SHARE

VIDEO

3 **IN GROUPS** Watch the video and answer the question.

SYM What influences a person's character: family values or life experience?

In this unit, you will ...

- discuss possible devices that could help the lives of others, ask and answer questions about your achievements, and describe survival situations.
- use thinking skills: apply, evaluate, and analyze.
- read about technology for an accessible world.
- use strategies to start a discussion, use language to say you do not understand to repair a conversation, and justify reasons in a discussion.
- use decision-making skills to choose items and write a survival list.
- learn skills for effective time management.

Life-Changing Technology

READING

A **READING SKILL—Predict information** **Look at the picture. What do you think the article is going to be about?**

B **1.01 Read the article. Then answer the questions.**

Technology Creating an Accessible World

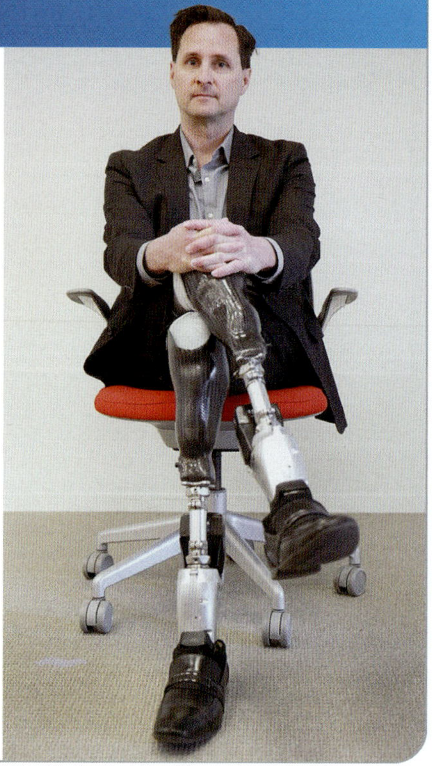

Through the use of technology, we are changing the world that is accessible to us. People such as Hugh Herr, co-director of the MIT Center for Extreme Bionics, are responsible for these changes. After losing both of his legs in a mountain climbing accident, Hugh Herr designed and developed new bionic legs. These new legs have a number of features that were previously **impossible**. The legs can be made longer or shorter. The feet can change depending on the surface of the mountain. It is even possible to attach different climbing equipment. All of these advances mean that Hugh Herr can **achieve** climbs that no one else has ever been able to do before. The MIT Center for Extreme Bionics is currently working on a digital nervous system which will connect the brain with a computer that can control artificial arms and legs.

Another area in which connections with computers are having a huge effect is communication. Facebook is currently working on a "silent speech" project: computers that can **recognize** what people are thinking so they can type messages with their brain. This system can help people who are **disabled** because of **disease** or injury. It can also help **able-bodied** people who want a faster way to type their ideas. Early tests in similar systems have used a person's thoughts to **select** letters and then write words. However, systems will get much faster. The aim of the silent speech project is for thoughts to be **turned into** text at a speed of 100 words per minute. How would you use technology to access a whole new world?

GLOSSARY

artificial (adj): made by people and used instead of something natural
accessible (adj): when a place or object can be easily used by all.

1 What technology did Hugh Herr develop? ____________________
2 What is special about that technology? ____________________
3 How else can systems that connect people to computers help us? ____________________
4 What advantages of these systems are mentioned in the text? ____________________

____

C **THINKING SKILL—Apply** **Explain how technology improves your ability to work, travel, socialize, and study.**

VOCABULARY

A **Match the words in bold in READING B with the definitions (1–8).**

1 ____________ (phr v): made one thing become another
2 ____________ (adj): unable to use part of your body in the way most other people can
3 ____________ (adj): not possible
4 ____________ (v): chooses
5 ____________ (v): know what you are seeing because you have seen it before
6 ____________ (adj): able to use your body in the way most other people can
7 ____________ (v): be successful, usually after hard work
8 ____________ (n): illness

GRAMMAR stative and dynamic verbs

A Complete the sentences from the text in READING A.

1 Through the use of technology, we ______ the world that is accessible to us.
2 These new legs ______ a number of features that were previously impossible.
3 Another area in which connections with computers ______ a huge effect is communication.
4 Computers that can recognize what people ______ so they can type messages with their brain.

B Read the sentences in A and choose the correct options.

1 Stative verbs, e.g., *know*, *have*, and *like*, describe **actions** / **states**.
2 Dynamic verbs, e.g., *write*, *walk*, and *use*, describe **actions** / **states**.
3 **Stative** / **Dynamic** verbs are not usually used in progressive tenses.
4 Some verbs, e.g., *be*, *have*, and *think*, can be used both ways with **the same** / **a different** meaning.

For more practice, go to page 142.

C Check (✓) the correct sentences. Both sentences may be correct.

1 ☐ Do you know how disabled people use technology?
  ☐ Are you knowing anything about technology and disability?
2 ☐ I'm not understanding how the technology will help people.
  ☐ I don't understand what you're saying.
3 ☐ What do you think we can do to improve people's lives?
  ☐ What were you thinking about before this lesson began?
4 ☐ Do you have any problems that technology could solve?
  ☐ Are you having any problems with what I'm saying?

D IN PAIRS Ask and answer the questions.

1 What careers do you know that involve working with disabled people?
2 Which of those careers do you think would be most suitable for you?

MAKE IT REAL

Some people might use verbs such as *like* and *love* with progressive tenses, e.g., *Are you liking your new apartment? Yes, I'm loving it!* This makes the statement more intense. Remember, though, that some people don't think it's correct.

SPEAKING

A IN PAIRS Decide which of these pieces of technology you think would make the most difference in people's lives. Say why.

- a device that knows what you are thinking about and says the words aloud
- a device that knows what you are looking at and recreates the image on a computer screen

B Think of another device that would help the lives of others. Draw a simple picture or write a short explanation. Tell the class about your device. Use the Confident Communicator box to help you.

CONFIDENT COMMUNICATOR
START TALKING

To start a discussion, use *What do you think about …*
What do you think about a device to help people with reading?

Amazing Abilities

VOCABULARY noun suffixes

A Complete the table with words from the box and nouns formed from the words.

achieve	develop	impossible	responsible
argue	hard	kind	sad
available	ill	possible	

Verb + *–ment*	Adjective + *–ness*	Adjective ending in *–able/–ible* + *–ity*
entertain–entertainment	*happy–happiness*	*able–ability*

B IN PAIRS Ask and answer the questions.

1 What do you think your greatest achievement is?
2 What was the last argument you had? What happened?

LISTENING

A 1.02 You are going to listen to part of a lecture. Look at the pictures and say why you think these two people might be mentioned in the lecture. Listen and check.

Wolfgang Amadeus Mozart (1756–1791)

Daniel Tammet (1979–)

B 1.02 LISTENING SKILL—Recognize signposts Listen again and complete the sentences.

1 Over the ________ few lectures, we looked at …
2 To ________ with, people with perfect pitch can …
3 As you ________ know, Mozart could play …
4 Moving ________ to language learning, we all have …

C 1.02 Listen again and complete the notes with the relevant numbers.

1 People with perfect pitch: 1 in ________
2 Mozart played violin and keyboard, age ________
3 Mozart wrote symphony, age ________
4 Daniel Tammet speaks ________ languages.
5 David Tammet learned Icelandic in ________ week.

D THINKING SKILL—Evaluate Consider how Daniel Tammet was able to learn Icelandic so quickly.

GRAMMAR expressing ability

A Match the sentences (1–5) with the correct explanations of the language of ability (a–c). You will use some explanations more than once.

1 People with perfect pitch **can** hear a musical note and tell you exactly what it is. ______
2 Mozart **could** play the violin and the keyboard at the age of five. ______
3 And he **managed to** write his first symphony at the age of eight. ______
4 And many of us **have succeeded in** learning one or two foreign languages. ______
5 Some people **are able to** learn languages amazingly quickly. ______

a a general ability in the present
b a general ability in the past
c an ability that has been achieved despite difficulty

For more practice, go to page 142.

B Choose the correct options.

1 Some people … speak more than one language.
a don't succeed in **b** aren't able to **c** don't manage
2 How many languages … now?
a can you speak **b** could you speak **c** did you manage to speak
3 After a lot of practice, I finally … to learn how to play the piano.
a succeeded **b** could **c** managed
4 I … ride a bike by the time I was six.
a managed **b** can **c** could
5 Even though my brother has perfect pitch, he … becoming a professional musician.
a couldn't **b** wasn't able to **c** didn't succeed in

C IN PAIRS Tell your partner one thing you managed to do this week.

PRONUNCIATION word stress with *–ity*

A 1.03 Underline the stressed syllable in each word. Listen, check, and practice.

1 able ability
2 available availability

SPEAKING

A Think of a time when you did something that was hard, e.g., passed an exam, learned a new skill, etc. Make notes about any details you remember.

B IN PAIRS Ask and answer the questions about your achievements. Use the Confident Communicator box to help you.

1 Do you have an achievement you are proud of?
2 How did you manage to do it?
3 What did you do in the beginning? How did you feel?
4 What did you manage to do that helped you?
5 How did that help you? What were you able to do then?
6 What happened in the end?

CONFIDENT COMMUNICATOR
REPAIR IT

When you don't understand something, use the following phrases to repair the conversation:
Sorry, what was that?
I'm sorry—I didn't understand what you said.
What do you mean by personal achievements?

Three Stories of Survival

VOCABULARY character adjectives

A Find and underline the negative character adjective. Use a dictionary if necessary.

brave	confident	curious	independent	reliable
calm	creative	generous	selfish	

MAKE IT YOURS

Do these adjectives describe you? What other words could you use to describe your character?

B Write an adjective from the box for each description.

1 Danielle never thinks about other people's feelings. ________________
2 Lauren isn't afraid of anything. She likes dangerous situations! ________________
3 Kyle never seems to be nervous. He really believes in himself. ________________
4 Juan Carlos will happily give you money if you need some. ________________
5 Madison always wants to know more about things and asks lots of questions. ________________
6 Joshua doesn't like asking for help and wants to do things himself. ________________
7 Sophie never gets angry or worried. She always seems to be relaxed. ________________
8 Chelsea always does what she says she will. She won't disappoint you. ________________

LISTENING

A Look at B. Before you listen, predict what kind of information you need to write.

B 1.04 LISTENING SKILL—Listen for specific information
Listen to a podcast. Then complete the notes with a number, word, or short phrase.

1 Born: ________________
2 Crash happened when she was: ________________
3 Height of plane: ________________
4 Saved by: ________________
5 Food: ________________
6 In rain forest for: ________________
7 Later, became: ________________
8 *When I Fell From the Sky* published in: ________________

Juliane Koepcke

C 1.04 THINKING SKILL—Analyze Listen again and explain why you think Juliane followed a stream.

WRITING a blog post

A Read the blog post and choose *True* or *False*.

AN AMAZING STORY

Hi, guys! I want to share with you an amazing story of survival. Some of you might know about it already. In 2018, 12 teenagers and their football coach went into caves in Thailand. It started to rain and they couldn't get out because of the water. They were in there for nine days without any food or light. They drank water from the cave walls! Divers managed to find them after a long search, but they still had a problem. The water made it very hard to get the boys out, and most of them couldn't swim. And it was the start of the rainy season, so they didn't have a lot of time. Finally, the divers succeeded in getting all the boys out, but it wasn't easy.

I hate the idea of being stuck in a dark cave! I'd be very scared. You need to be calm and independent to survive a situation like that. I think the boys were really brave, and so were the divers who rescued them. They had to be creative to find a solution to the problem, but they did it. If you are curious, search online and read the whole story.

The writer …

1 speaks directly to the readers to create a friendly style. True / False
2 gives his or her personal reaction and then describes what happened. True / False
3 explains what problems different people faced. True / False
4 imagines himself or herself in the survival situation. True / False
5 gives his or her opinion of the people in the situation. True / False
6 tells readers to write their own blog posts. True / False

B Choose the correct spelling.

1 **a** surviveal **b** survival
2 **a** achievement **b** achievment
3 **a** possibileity **b** possibility
4 **a** amazement **b** amazment
5 **a** amazeing **b** amazing

C Make notes about a story of survival. You can use the story in LISTENING B, the story in WRITING A, or another story of survival you know about.

1 When did this happen? ______
2 Who was involved? ______
3 What happened first? ______
4 Then what happened? ______
5 What happened in the end? ______
6 What's your reaction? ______
7 What do you think of the people involved? ______

D Write a blog post about a story of survival.

SPEAKING

A Choose one of these survival situations. Make notes.

a hurricane

an earthquake

a flood

How I would feel:

______

______

What I would do:

______

______

B IN PAIRS Tell your partner about the survival situation you have chosen. Then ask and answer the questions. Use the Confident Communicator box to help you.

1 What personal qualities does it take to survive in a hard situation?
2 Do you think you have those personal qualities?

CONFIDENT COMMUNICATOR
KEEP TALKING

To justify reasons in a discussion, it helps to describe your feelings and explain your choices:
In a hurricane / an earthquake / a flood, I would feel nervous and frightened.
I'd hate to be in a hurricane / an earthquake / a flood because it would be very frightening.

Language and Life

Decision Making – Survival Situation

A 1.05 **Read the description. Then answer the questions.**

Surviving in the Desert

It is 9 o'clock in the morning on a warm July day. You and your three colleagues were on a short flight to a conference in Southern California when your plane developed mechanical problems. The plane was forced off course by a few miles. Finally, the mechanical problems got worse, the pilot lost control of the plane, and you all crash-landed in the desert. You and your three colleagues find yourselves quite far from the plane. Although you keep looking, unfortunately it seems that the pilot is missing. You and your colleagues are on your own.

The nearest town, which you saw from the window when you flew over it half an hour ago, is about 30 kilometers away. That is an extremely long walk, and you know that it will be very difficult. None of you can get any signal at all on your cell phones, and without signal, none of the apps work. Daytime temperatures in this area can reach 40°C, and at night, they can fall below 0°C. It is already starting to get very warm, and you know that soon you will be in danger. One of your colleagues remembers reading an article about the desert, and he says it is better to move around during the evening, because it is less hot. He says that between late afternoon and sunset is the best time to move.

In different parts of the desert around you, you see a variety of different things, including a map, an empty lighter, and a few items of clothing. You discuss ideas with your colleagues and as you talk, you realize that you need to come up with a plan if you are going to manage to survive. Suddenly, there is a smell of smoke in the air. You look towards the plane and you see that it is beginning to catch fire. You know that this means that there is not much time to decide what to do because the fuel in the plane's tanks could explode. What do you do?

1 How would you feel in a situation like this? ____________________

2 What skills do you think you would need in a situation like this? ____________________

____

3 What are the main problems you and your group face? ____________________

____

B IN GROUPS **Look at the items you have recovered from the crash. Decide how important each one is to you. Number them from 1 (most important) to 8 (least important). How might you use each item? Make sure everyone in your group agrees.**

lighter

clothes

map of the area

chocolate bars

mirror

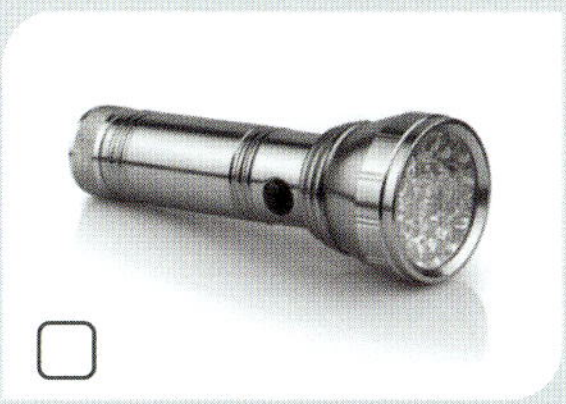

flashlight

radio

container of water

C Write your top four items from B. Explain to the class what they are and why you have chosen them instead of the other items. Take turns to explain an item so that each person in your group gets to speak. Leave the scores for each item until later.

Top 4 items:

1 ____________________ Score: _____ **3** ____________________ Score: _____

2 ____________________ Score: _____ **4** ____________________ Score: _____

D Complete each sentence with an object from B. Then calculate the scores for your choices in C.

The best survival strategy is to stay where you are. Each pilot files a flight plan before taking off, and so rescuers will follow that when the flight doesn't arrive at your destination. The worst strategy is to set off to try to reach the town. You would be unlikely to get there before becoming exhausted. Therefore, the **1** ____________________ is not very useful: 0 points. The **2** ____________________ is also unlikely to be much help, because you can only receive a signal, not send one: 0 points. The **3** ____________________ will be useful when the temperature drops at night: 5 points. The **4** ____________________ will make a spark and can be used to start a fire: 10 points. The **5** ____________________ will provide you with some energy and are easy to digest: 10 points. The **6** ____________________ is useful for signaling at night: 10 points. The **7** ____________________ is essential for when you get thirsty: 15 points. The **8** ____________________ is also extremely important. You can use it to reflect the sun to signal to any rescuers: 15 points.

E Add the scores of each of your top four items and record your total score.

Total Score	
45–65	Congratulations! You've got great survival skills. You are finally rescued when you are able to signal a plane overhead. Perhaps your adventures have given you a taste for the great outdoors!
35–45	Good job. It wasn't easy, but you succeeded in getting the attention of the rescuers. Think twice before going out into the wilderness again.
Less than 35	Uh-oh. It looks like the desert was the winner this time. You need to think clearly and stay calm if you're going to come out on top next time!

F Discuss the questions.

1 What approach did you use to decide which items to choose?
2 In what other situations might you use this approach?

MAKE IT DIGITAL

Go online and find other stories of survival. How did those people survive and what did they use?

VOCABULARY review

SCORE: / 10

A Complete the sentences with words from the box. There are three words you don't need.

able-bodied brave calm creative curious disabled reliable selfish

1 If you are ________________, you are good at making things or coming up with new ideas.
2 If you are ________________, you are unable to use part of your body.
3 If you are ________________, you don't care about other people.
4 If you are ________________, you have courage and you are not afraid.
5 If you are ________________, you want to know more about a subject.

B Complete the sentences with nouns.

1 Jack took a lot of days off work last year because of ________________ (ill).
2 I like working here because there are opportunities for professional ________________ (develop).
3 Is there any ________________ (possible) that you're wrong about this issue?
4 I had an ________________ (argue) with the janitor because I couldn't get into the building in my wheelchair.
5 My greatest ________________ (achieve) is learning to climb again after my accident.

GRAMMAR review

SCORE: / 10

A Choose the correct words and phrases.

The *Jascon-4*, a small boat, went down in heavy seas near Nigeria on May 26, 2013. No one **1 thought / was thinking** that there were any survivors. However, one man, Harrison Odjegba Okene, the ship's cook, managed **2 surviving / to survive**. At a depth of 30 meters, it was totally dark and he **3 can't / couldn't** see a thing. He **4 knew / was knowing** that he needed to find a safe space. Time **5 ran / was running** out, but luckily, he succeeded **6 to find / in finding** a pocket of air in the engineer's office. It **7 can / is able** be dangerous in cold water, but he was able **8 make / to make** a small platform from a mattress that kept his upper body out of the water. He was there for three days. Finally, he **9 can / could** hear a noise. It was the divers who **10 searched / were searching** for the boat. He was rescued, but he said he would never go to sea again!

16–20 correct: You can describe people's characters and form nouns with suffixes.
You can use stative and dynamic verbs and express ability.
0–15 correct: Look again at the Vocabulary and Grammar sections in the unit.

TOTAL SCORE: / 20

WHAT DO YOU KNOW NOW? Look back at page 7 and add the words you know now to the boxes.

STUDY SKILLS EFFECTIVE TIME MANAGEMENT

Take the quiz about effective time management. Go to **Study Skills** on page 127 to find the answers. Then learn more about effective time management.

1 Which two of the following are useful time management strategies?
a regularly checking your email **b** prioritizing what is important **c** making a detailed study plan

2 Rewarding yourself at the end of a study session will not help your motivation.
a True **b** False

3 Which of the following is likely to prevent effective time management?
a clarifying how you currently use your time **b** discussing challenges and solutions with other students **c** being surrounded by distractions

4 Effective time management skills are only really useful in academic settings.
a True **b** False

UNIT 2 The Animal Connection

WHAT DO YOU ALREADY KNOW?

1 Think about animals you know and their characteristics. Write the names of the animals.

2 **IN PAIRS** Share and compare your ideas. Add more words to your list.

Domestic animals / Characteristics

Wild animals / Characteristics

VIDEO

DISCUSS & SHARE

3 **IN GROUPS** **Watch the video and answer the question.**

SYM Are you a dog person or a cat person?

In this unit, you will ...

- talk about intelligent animals, discuss possible jobs with animals, and make arguments for and against owning exotic pets.
- use thinking skills: recall, analyze, and evaluate.
- read about animals and the mirror test for intelligence.
- use strategies and language to move on to your next point, start a conversation about hypothetical situations, and disagree politely.
- use problem-solving skills to find solutions to help stray animals.
- follow a wildlife photographer to learn about this job and the skills needed for this industry.

READING

A **Apart from humans, which animals do you think are intelligent?**

B 2.01 **Read the blog post. Then choose *True* or *False*.**

The Mirror Test

Animals are interesting, aren't they? They can be **cute**, they can be fast, and they can be strong. But are they **intelligent**?

That isn't an easy question to answer. Animals all live in different habitats and their **behavior** is right for that situation. We need a standard way to test an animal's behavior. The mirror test, developed in 1970 by Dr. Gordon Gallup Jr., gives us that.

You recognize your own reflection in a mirror, don't you? But does an animal know that it's looking at itself when it looks in a mirror, or does it think it's a different animal? If an animal passes the mirror test, there's a good chance it is intelligent. We give the animal medicine so it goes to sleep. Then, we put a colored mark on the animal's body where it can't see it in a normal way, such as on its forehead or on its ear. When the animal wakes up and sees itself in a mirror, we watch how it behaves.

Animals that pass the mirror test see the mark and touch it or try to remove it. So far, the species that have passed the test are great apes (chimpanzees, bonobos, and orangutans), elephants, dolphins, orcas, and Eurasian magpies. Some people say, though, that the test only works with animals that mainly use **sight** to explore the world, and it may not be a fair test of other animals, such as dogs, who use **smell** or sound more than sight and fail the test.

GLOSSARY

habitat (n): place where an animal naturally lives

1. An animal's environment changes how it acts. True / False
2. The mirror test is done while the animal is asleep. True / False
3. In the mirror test, the animal puts color on its body using the mirror. True / False
4. Animals pass the mirror test if they know they are looking at themselves. True / False

C **READING SKILL—Understand examples** **Find and write examples from the text in B.**

1. a good place to put a mark on an animal for the mirror test ______________________
2. an animal that passes the mirror test ______________________
3. an animal that fails the mirror test ______________________

D **THINKING SKILL—Recall** **Without reading the text again, describe how the mirror test works.**

VOCABULARY

A **Complete the definitions (1–5) with the words in bold in READING B.**

1. The sense of ______________ is very important to animals that hunt with their eyes, such as cats.
2. The sense of ______________ is very important to animals that use their noses a lot, such as bears.
3. An ______________ person is good at understanding difficult ideas.
4. An animal's ______________ is the way it acts and the things it does.
5. People often think that baby animals, such as kittens and puppies, are ______________.

GRAMMAR tag questions

A Read the tag questions and choose the correct options.

Animals are interesting, aren't they?

You recognize your own reflection in a mirror, don't you?

1. To form a tag question with the verb *be*, we use the verb **be** / **do** and an appropriate pronoun.
2. To form a tag question with other verbs, we use the verb **be** / **do** and an appropriate pronoun.
3. To form a tag question with a modal, **use the verb *be*** / **repeat the modal**.
4. When the verb in the main part of the sentence is positive, the verb in the tag is **negative** / **positive**.

For more practice, go to page 143.

B Complete the tag questions.

1. You're James, ______________________________?
2. It's cold today, ______________________________?
3. Jack's a really smart dog, ______________________________?
4. Horses are very intelligent, ______________________________?
5. Dolphins can be taught tricks, ______________________________?
6. Your mom works with animals, ______________________________?

MAKE IT REAL

In informal situations, some people might use *right* at the end of a sentence instead of using a tag question, e.g., *You're a vet, **right**?*

SPEAKING

A Put the animals in order of intelligence from 1 (most intelligent) to 5 (least intelligent).

_____

_____

_____

_____

_____

B IN PAIRS Tell each other what order you have put the animals in. Explain your reasons. Use the Confident Communicator box to help you.

A: Parrots can talk, can't they? I think that means they're smart.

B: Maybe, but dolphins are smarter, aren't they? They can learn lots of tricks.

CONFIDENT COMMUNICATOR

KEEP TALKING

Use the following phrases to move on to your next point for discussion.

***What about** horses? Do you think they're intelligent?*

***Let's move on to** rabbits. Are they intelligent?*

***Next, let's think about** parrots. They're intelligent, aren't they?*

LESSON 2 **Working With Animals**

VOCABULARY careers with animals

A Check (✓) the careers you need a degree to do.

☐ dog handler

☐ vet/veterinarian

☐ zookeeper

☐ wildlife photographer

☐ breeder

☐ marine biologist

☐ horse trainer

☐ zoologist

B IN PAIRS Decide which career(s) from A would be most appropriate for Holly.

Holly is 18 and is considering a career with animals. She loves small animals and has always had a number of pets. She has good exam results, but she would rather take a practical course than an academic course.

LISTENING

A What do you think this person is doing?

B 2.02 LISTENING SKILLS—Use key information to predict content Listen to Part 1 of a talk. Then check what topics you expect to hear in the rest of the talk.

- ☐ academic qualifications
- ☐ salary
- ☐ work experience
- ☐ personal qualities

C 2.03 Listen to Part 2 of the talk. Then complete the sentences.

1. A marine biologist is someone who studies animals that live __________________.
2. Some marine biologists do __________________ in the summer months.
3. To be a marine biologist, you'll need a __________________ in biology or marine biology.
4. The person who gets venom from a snake is known as a __________________.
5. Venom is used to make antivenom for when a snake __________________.

D THINKING SKILL—Analyze Decide what kind of person would make a good snake milker. Say whether you think you would be good at that job.

GRAMMAR articles

A Match the sentence beginnings (1–3) with the ends (a–c).

A marine biologist is someone who studies animals that live in the sea.
A snake milker takes venom from a snake. The venom is very useful.

1 We use the indefinite article (*a*, *an*) _____
2 We use the definite article (*the*) _____
3 We use no article _____

a with singular countable nouns, with plural countable nouns when we are being specific, and when there is only one of something (*the sun, the sky, etc.*).
b with plural countable nouns and uncountable nouns when we are talking generally.
c with singular countable nouns when we are not being specific or when we mention something for the first time.

For more practice, go to page 144.

B Complete the sentences with *a*, *an*, or *the*. If no article is needed, put an X.

When **1** ____________ director needs **2** ____________ animal for **3** ____________ movie, they turn to **4** ____________ animal trainer. **5** ____________ animal trainer then provides **6** ____________ trained animal to do whatever **7** ____________ director wants them to do. But what does it take to become **8** ____________ animal trainer?
Of course, you need to enjoy working with **9** ____________ animals. More than that, though, you have to be interested in **10** ____________ animal behavior. You should also be in shape and able to work outdoors.

C IN PAIRS Say if you think you would be a good animal trainer.

PRONUNCIATION *the*

A 2.04 Listen to the sentences. What do you notice about the pronunciation of *the*?

I have to take my dog to the vet.
My dog has to stay in the animal hospital.

B Practice the sentence: I like to see the animals at the zoo.

SPEAKING

A Read the questions and make notes.

1 If you were going to work with animals, what kind of animals would you like to work with (small, large, marine, etc.)? ____________
2 What kind of place (lab, outdoors, etc.) would you like to work in? ____________
3 How closely would you like to work with animals? ____________

B IN PAIRS Talk about your answers to the questions in A. Discuss what careers with animals each of you might enjoy. Use the Confident Communicator box to help you.

CONFIDENT COMMUNICATOR
START TALKING

To start a conversation about hypothetical situations, use the following phrases:
If I were going to work with animals, I would like to work with small animals, such as cats and dogs.
The animals I'd like to work with are marine animals.

Endangered Species

VOCABULARY animals

A Name the animals. Then check (✓) the ones you think are endangered.

- ☐ crocodile ☐ dolphin ☐ hippo ☐ polar bear ☐ porcupine
- ☐ puma ☐ shark ☐ tiger ☐ turtle ☐ whale

1  ______

2  ______

3  ______

4  ______

5  ______

6  ______

7  ______

8  ______

9  ______

10  ______

B IN PAIRS Compare your answers. Say why you think some of the animals are endangered.

LISTENING

A Have you visited a zoo? What was it like?

B 2.05 LISTENING SKILL—Listen for key words
Look at the word cloud. Listen to a presentation and circle words and phrases you hear.

mammal reptile natural tourism the wild zoo habitat hunter wildlife endangered animal conservation creature climate tropical danger species nature environment

C 2.05 Listen again and choose the correct options.

1 The zoo tries to make ...
   a the zoo environment as natural as possible.
   b animals behave in different ways.

2 The zoo wants to educate people about ...
   a the work the zookeepers do with the animals.
   b the problems some animals face in the wild.

3 The zoo's breeding program ...
   a provides animals for other zoos.
   b aims to help endangered species in the wild.

D THINKING SKILL—Evaluate What arguments can you think of against zoos? Choose the most persuasive points.

WRITING an opinion post

A Read the arguments for and against supporting zoos. Then answer the questions in your notebook.

Should we support zoos in the work that they do?

Zoos do a lot of good work. First of all, they educate the public. This inspires the next generation of zookeepers, vets, and environmentalists. In addition, zoos help to protect endangered species through the breeding work they do. Last, zoos are involved in environmental programs of different kinds around the world. We need to support our zoos.

Alessa, Lima, Peru

Zoos are cruel and unnecessary. To start with, animals in captivity are bored and cannot behave naturally. Many animals find being on display very stressful. What's more, some animals die younger in zoos than they would in the wild. Last but not least, zoos care more about baby animals, which attract paying visitors. We should not support zoos.

Jacob, New York, US

1 What are the main arguments given in favor of zoos?
2 What are the main arguments given against zoos?

B Write words and phrases from A that have the same meaning as these words and phrases.

first: **1** ______________________, **2** ______________________
also: **3** ______________________, **4** ______________________
finally: **5** ______________________, **6** ______________________

C You are going to write a post for the website on the following statement. Make notes to answer the questions.

We should close all zoos and release the animals into the wild.

1 Are you going to argue for or against this statement? ______________________
2 What is your main argument? ______________________
3 What other arguments do you want to mention? ______________________

D Write an opinion post for the website arguing either for or against the statement. Use the phrases from B to structure your post.

SPEAKING

A Think of arguments for and against allowing people to own exotic pets, such as tigers, chimpanzees, snakes, etc. Make notes.

Main arguments for:

____

Main arguments against:

____

B IN PAIRS Do you think people should be allowed to keep wild animals as pets? Why or why not?

C Tell the rest of the class what you talked about. How many of you are for and how many of you are against the idea? Use the Confident Communicator box to help you.

CONFIDENT COMMUNICATOR
KEEP TALKING

To disagree with someone politely, use *Yes, but …*
I think people should have the right to own exotic pets if they want to.
***Yes, but** what about the animals? Don't they have rights, too?*

Language and Life

Problem Solving – Strays

A 2.06 Read the article. Then answer the questions.

The Trouble With Strays

Puppies are cute, aren't they? And kittens are adorable. But those puppies and kittens grow up to be adult dogs and cats. Often the demands of being a pet owner just get to be too much for people and the cats and dogs end up on the street as strays. Sometimes it's the responsibility of looking after an adult animal that causes problems, and sometimes there are financial reasons. It's a growing problem. In the city of Detroit in the US, it is estimated that there are 50,000 stray dogs. The World Health Organization estimates that there are about 200 million stray dogs worldwide.

This situation causes a number of problems. First of all, the lives of stray animals are hard and stressful. Every day is a struggle to find enough to eat and a safe place to sleep. That means the animals are often in poor condition and get injured or die young. In addition to that, stray animals cause a number of problems for city residents. They can run into the road and cause traffic accidents. Stray animals can also carry diseases. They can pass these diseases on to people or to domestic pets. Last, packs of dogs can be dangerous and may attack people.

However, there may be a solution to the problem. One country that has reduced the number of stray dogs is the UK. In 2016, a new law was introduced. All dogs must be microchipped. This means that a small chip—the size of a grain of rice—is inserted under the dog's skin. It's a quick and painless procedure. Microchips contain a unique code that is connected to a national database. When the chip is scanned, it shows the owner's address. If your dog does not have a chip, you can receive a fine of up to £500. Microchipping is useful if your dog is lost or stolen, and it also encourages people to take more responsibility for their pets. According to the Dogs Trust's *Stray Dogs Survey Report*, in 2018, the number of stray animals in the UK was at its lowest level in 21 years—so this is a step in the right direction.

1 What are the causes of the stray animal problem? ______________________________

____

2 What problems do stray animals cause for city residents? ______________________________

____

3 How did the UK solve this problem? ______________________________

____

B IN GROUPS Talk about the situation in your own city or area. Check (✓) the main problems with animals and add details and ideas of your own.

Main animal problems in our city/area

☐ stray dogs
packs of dogs in some neighborhoods
____

☐ stray cats
____
____

☐ unwanted pets
____
____

☐ other problems
____
____

C **Read and assess the opinions. Do you think they are good suggestions? Why or why not?**

Amy2001	*We need more shelters. We should take the animals off the streets.*
CityGirl	*We should make sure the animals can't breed. And then release them back onto the streets.*
Ed_99	*We need to educate people more and stop the problem where it begins, in people's homes.*

A: Having more shelters is a good idea.
B: I agree, but maybe that's a short-term solution.

D **Brainstorm solutions for your city or area. Try to estimate the costs.**

Possible solutions for our city/area

Our estimated costs

E **Present your solutions to the class. Vote to choose the best ideas at a realistic cost.**

F **Discuss the questions.**

1. How did the costs of the solutions affect your choice?
2. What other factors did you consider when choosing solutions?
3. Why is it important to consider many factors when solving a problem?
4. What problems have you solved recently? How did you solve them?

MAKE IT DIGITAL

Find websites where people debate ideas. Read some of the posts and see what phrases they use for starting, for introducing further points, and for concluding.

VOCABULARY review

SCORE: / 10

A Complete the sentences with words from the box. There are two words you don't need.

apes	breeders	handlers	polar bears	species	wildlife
behavior	cute	hippos	sight	whales	zoologists

My job as a **1** ________________ photographer takes me all over the world. My main interest is in recording endangered **2** ________________ before they disappear. I've taken shots of **3** ________________ in the Arctic. That was dangerous because they aren't at all **4** ________________, cuddly creatures! They're real killers. I've also photographed **5** ________________ out at sea and I've taken shots of lions, **6** ________________, and zebras in Africa. My next project is to record the amazing **7** ________________ of the Asian jungles. I'd like to record their natural **8** ________________, as well as collect data that **9** ________________ will find useful. They have a good sense of hearing and a good sense of **10** ________________, particularly at night, so it won't be easy to find them!

GRAMMAR review

SCORE: / 10

A Check (✓) the correct tag questions. Rewrite the incorrect question tags.

1 ☐ Tigers are amazing animals, **aren't they**? ________________
2 ☐ You majored in marine biology, **don't you**? ________________
3 ☐ Gorillas will soon disappear in the wild, **will they**? ________________
4 ☐ We don't do enough to protect endangered species, **are we**? ________________
5 ☐ It's important to learn about nature in schools, **isn't it**? ________________

B Add five articles (*a*, *an*, *the*) to the text.

One of the most intelligent animals is the octopus. Octopuses can solve puzzles and can even open jar to get food. And when they solve puzzle, they can remember how to do it if they see puzzle again. Scientists estimate that octopus is about as intelligent as three-year-old child.

16–20 correct: You can talk about animals and people who work with animals. You can use tag questions and articles.
0–15 correct: Look again at the Vocabulary and Grammar sections in the unit.

TOTAL SCORE: / 20

WHAT DO YOU KNOW NOW? Look back at page 17 and add the words you know now to the boxes.

FOLLOW A PRO ANIMALS

Take the quiz about animals. Go to **Follow A Pro** on page 128 to find the answers. Then learn more about working with animals.

1 Where is the largest zoo in Mexico?
a Mexico City **b** Guadalajara **c** Puebla

2 How long is veterinary school in the US?
a one year **b** two years **c** four years

3 Approximately how many polar bears are there in the wild?
a 4,000 **b** 12,000 **c** 26,000

4 Which animal is the hippo most closely related to?
a whale **b** horse **c** dog

UNIT

3 Think About It

WHAT DO YOU ALREADY KNOW?

1 Think about words you know connected to thinking or skills. Write the words.

2 IN PAIRS Share and compare your ideas. Add more words to your lists.

Thinking/Skills

VIDEO

DISCUSS & SHARE

3 IN GROUPS Watch the video and answer the question.

SYM When do you think better: in the morning or in the evening?

In this unit, you will ...

- ask and answer questions about confirmation bias, discuss the importance of expert systems in your future career, and compare different creative uses for things.
- use thinking skills: analyze, evaluate, and apply.
- read about confirmation bias.
- use strategies and language to give yourself time to think, start a conversation, and ask for further suggestions.
- use design-thinking skills to design a new social media app.
- learn tips to create a presentation or give a talk.

READING

A **Do you think the world is generally getting better or getting worse? Why do you think that?**

B 3.01 **READING SKILL—Identify the topic** **Read the article. Then choose the best definition.**

a **confirmation bias (*n*):** the mistake we make when we don't think carefully enough about a subject and think that our first idea is correct

b **confirmation bias (*n*):** the thinking habit that means we accept evidence that supports the opinion we already have and don't accept other evidence

CONFIRMATION BIAS

Scientists believe that the average person receives about 34 gigabytes of information and sees or hears 100,500 words every day. That's a lot of information, and no one can possibly **concentrate on** all of it. We choose what we **pay attention to** and what we think is important. That creates a problem: confirmation bias. We like to be right, and so we listen to **evidence** that supports what we already believe and we **ignore** evidence that goes against what we believe. For example, if you believe that the world is generally getting worse, you will see only evidence to support your opinion when you hear the news. You will pay attention to stories about rising crime and environmental problems. And you will ignore evidence that suggests people around the world are getting richer, becoming healthier, and living longer.

Confirmation bias means we see what we want to see. It can create problems. For instance, a business may try a new strategy. The managers will notice positive results, such as increased sales, before they notice negative ones, such as increased costs. That could be expensive for the business. Social media and other websites can make confirmation bias worse. Groups of online friends often agree with each other. They easily share information and news stories that support their opinions. They **rarely** hear the other side of the argument and miss **relevant** information. Some people are worried that this kind of "social media bubble" is bad for society.

Is there anything you can do to question your own confirmation bias? You can **make an effort** to listen to people with different views. You can visit websites that present a different opinion from yours. As soon as you do that, you will learn something about how other people think.

C **Write short answers to the questions.**

1 What is the cause of confirmation bias? ______

2 Why might confirmation bias cause problems for a business? ______

3 Why can social media make confirmation bias worse? ______

4 What can you do to prevent confirmation bias? ______

D **THINKING SKILL—Analyze** **Explain other ways in which confirmation bias could be a problem.**

VOCABULARY

A **Complete the sentences with the words and phrases in bold in READING B.**

1 If you ______ the lecturer, you will understand the topic better.

2 People ______ listen carefully to other people's opinions—in fact, they almost never do!

3 Please don't ______ me! Listen to what I'm saying.

4 What ______ do you have that supports your opinion?

5 I know learning to play an instrument is hard, but if you ______, you'll improve.

6 I like to collect all the ______ information before I make an important decision.

7 I can't ______ my work with all this noise!

GRAMMAR future time clauses (*after, as soon as, before, until, when*)

A Choose the correct option.

1 You will see only evidence to support your opinion when … the news.
  a you hear **b** you will hear
2 The managers will notice positive results before … negative ones.
  a they notice **b** they will notice

B Choose the correct options.

1 We **use** / **don't use** the future tense in a time clause.
2 We use the **simple present** / **simple past** in the time clause.

For more practice, go to page 144.

C Complete the sentences.

1 I __________ (call) you as soon as I __________ (get) home.
2 From now on, I __________ (not share) a story on social media until I __________ (check) it.
3 I think the problem __________ (get) worse before it __________ (get) better.
4 __________ (you / meet) me at the airport when I __________ (arrive)?
5 After I __________ (watch) the movie, I __________ (tell) you whether I like it or not.

D IN PAIRS Ask and answer the questions.

1 What will you do when this lesson ends?
2 What will you do as soon as you get home tonight?

MAKE IT REAL

We also use time clauses with *the minute* or *the instant*, meaning "immediately," e.g., *Call me* ***the minute*** *you get there.*

SPEAKING

A Make notes. You do not need to write complete sentences.

1 Do you and your online friends always agree about things or do you sometimes disagree? What do you disagree about?
____
2 In what ways do you think confirmation bias is a problem?
____
3 Now that you've read about confirmation bias, will you do anything different when you are online?
____

B IN PAIRS Ask and answer the questions in A. Use the Confident Communicator box to help you.

CONFIDENT COMMUNICATOR
KEEP TALKING

Use the following phrases to give yourself time to think when asked a question.
That's a good question.
Let me think about that for a minute.

LESSON 2 Artificial Intelligence

LISTENING

A **Do you think machines will be able to think in the future?**

B **3.02 LISTENING SKILL—Listen for attitude** **Listen to a radio call-in show. Match the callers (1–4) to the statements (a–d).**

1 Julia: ______ **a** This person is confident that AI makes the world safer.
2 Rafael: ______ **b** This person is afraid that AI will change the economy.
3 Megan: ______ **c** This person is doubtful that machines will ever be intelligent.
4 Victor: ______ **d** This person is worried that AI might get out of control.

C **3.02** **Listen to the call-in show again. Then complete the sentences.**

1 Julia says that machines are just ______________ when they play games such as chess.
2 Julia says that humans are good at thinking because they have been doing it for ______________.
3 Rafael says that humans make mistakes because they get ______________.
4 Megan says that ______________ how some computer systems work and that's dangerous.
5 Victor says that machines may do ______________ of American jobs in the future.
6 Victor says that people who work ______________ may lose their jobs.

D **THINKING SKILLS—Evaluate** **Consider and describe other ways we use AI today.**

VOCABULARY word formation

A **Complete the table with the different forms of the words. Check your ideas in pairs.**

Verb	Adjective	Noun (abstract)	Noun (person)
create	1 ______	5 ______ 6 ______	11 ______
power	2 ______ 3 ______	power	
solve	solvable	7 ______	solver
think		8 ______	thinker
	4 ______	danger	
employ	employable	9 ______ 10 ______	12 ______ 13 ______

B **IN PAIRS** **Discuss the questions.**

1 As computers get more powerful, is there a danger to employment from AI?
2 Will computers ever be powerful enough to understand emotions?

PRONUNCIATION *say, says, said*

A **3.03** **How do we say each of the words in bold? Listen, check, and practice.**

1 Some people **say** that AI is a danger.
2 My mom **says** that she'll never lose her job to a robot.
3 My dad **said** the same thing and then lost his job!

GRAMMAR present perfect progressive

A **Read the sentences from LISTENING B and complete the explanation.**

Scientists have been researching artificial intelligence since the 1950s.
Humans have been thinking and solving problems for 200,000 years.
I've been thinking about AI a lot recently.

We form the present perfect progressive with *has/have* + ______________ + ______________.

B **Read the sentences in A again and choose the correct option.**

1. We use the present perfect progressive to talk about …
   a an activity that started in the past and is still in progress now.
   b an experience at a particular time in the past.
2. We also use the present perfect progressive to talk about …
   a the result of a recent continuing action.
   b an experience at any time in the past.
3. To talk about a finished action in the past that has results in the present, we use …
   a the present perfect.
   b the present perfect progressive.
4. When we mention the point the action began, we use **for** / **since**.
5. When we mention the duration of the action, we use **for** / **since**.

For more practice, go to page 145.

C **Complete the sentences.**

Expert Systems

An expert system is a computer program that uses AI to solve problems. People in various professions have **1** ____________ using expert systems **2** ____________ a number of years. An expert system uses a database of knowledge together with rules for using that knowledge. Scientists **3** ____________ been using them **4** ____________ 1965, when the first expert system was developed. Many health professionals, such as doctors and nurses, use expert systems. Health professionals **5** ____________ been recording our health data **6** ____________ the day we were born. Perhaps your doctor **7** ____________ been using one **8** ____________ some time to help decide what is wrong with his or her patients. Expert systems are just one of the ways in which AI **9** ____________ been helping people in the workplace. Where else do you think expert systems are used?

D **IN PAIRS Ask and answer the questions.**

1. How have people been using AI recently?
2. What have you been doing in another class / at work recently?
3. How long have you been living where you live now?

SPEAKING

A **Think about your chosen career and answer the questions.**

1. Are expert systems used in your chosen career now? In what ways?
2. Do you think expert systems will be used more in your chosen career in the future? In what ways?
3. Do you think your chosen career is in danger from expert systems or AI? Why or why not?

B **IN PAIRS Ask and answer the questions in A.**

A: I'm planning to be a lawyer in future. I think that lawyers have been using expert systems for years to research past cases.

B: Do you think that lawyers will use expert systems more in the future?

CONFIDENT COMMUNICATOR

START TALKING

To start your conversation, use the following phrases:

I'm planning to be a doctor.

I'm hoping to work as an engineer.

I want to work in accounting.

VOCABULARY phrasal verbs

A Match the phrasal verbs in bold (1–6) to the definitions (a–f).

1 How do you **come up with** all your amazing ideas? _____
2 You should never **give up** if you want to achieve your dreams. _____
3 Why don't you **look up** the word in an online dictionary? _____
4 Don't **make up** excuses! I know you broke my phone! _____
5 You can **rely on** this smartphone. It'll never break down or stop working. _____
6 I might **take up** a new sport to try to get in shape. _____

a stop making an effort
b find information in a book or online
c write or say something that isn't true
d think of, create
e start doing a regular activity, a hobby, etc.
f trust someone or something to do what they should do

MAKE IT YOURS
There are many different ways to describe how you have ideas. How could you describe the way you have ideas?

B IN PAIRS Choose the answers that are true for you. Talk to your partner about your choices.

1 I find it **easy** / **hard** to come up with ideas.
2 I **often** / **sometimes** / **never** give up if I find things hard.
3 I **often** / **sometimes** / **never** look things up to check information.
4 I **often** / **sometimes** / **never** make things up and I **always** / **don't always** tell the truth.
5 I **often** / **sometimes** / **never** rely on other people.
6 I **often** / **sometimes** / **never** take up a new activity.

LISTENING

A Discuss when it is important or useful to think creatively.

B 3.04 Listen to Part 1 of a talk and choose *True* or *False*.

1 Some people always find it easy to be creative. True / False
2 Some people will never be creative. True / False
3 Knowledge stops you from being creative. True / False
4 Feeling like a new learner helps creativity. True / False

C 3.05 LISTENING SKILL—Listen for main ideas Listen to Part 2 of the talk. Make notes about the three creative exercises the speaker describes.

Exercise 1: ______
Exercise 2: ______
Exercise 3: ______

GLOSSARY
fictional (adj): invented for a book, play, or movie

D THINKING SKILL—Apply Record as many different ways to use a paper clip as you can. You have three minutes.

WRITING an informal email

A Read the email. Then answer the questions.

New Message

To: Cc Bcc

Subject:

a Hi Alex.

Sorry I didn't reply to you sooner. **b** I've been working a lot, but it isn't so bad now.

We had a talk at work about being productive, and **c** I thought you would be interested in it. The speaker said we can all be productive, and he gave us a few tips.

d First of all, it's a good idea to have a to-do list. It really helps you to keep going when you just feel like giving up! And it also helps you to focus on what you're doing.

e The second thing he mentioned is the 2-Minute Rule. When you can't start something, choose a task that will take two minutes. Everyone has two minutes to do something. And when you start, it's easy to continue!

f Hope you find this useful.

g Regards,

h Grace

Send

1. What reason does Grace give for not writing?
2. What did Grace do at work?
3. How does a to-do list help?
4. How does the 2-Minute Rule help?

B Match the descriptions (1–8) with the correct parts of the email in A (a–h).

1. the second main point ______
2. a closing expression such as *Love*, *Best wishes*, etc. ______
3. a piece of personal news ______
4. a general description of the rest of the email ______
5. the writer's first name ______
6. a short wish or hope ______
7. a greeting with *Hi* or *Dear* ______
8. the first main point ______

C Write an email to a friend. Describe the talk in LISTENING B. Use the email in A as a model.

SPEAKING

A Write one more object in each list. Make sure that the objects you add are different from the ones already listed.

List A	List B
a pineapple	a guitar
a fork	a ladder
a cell phone	a clock
______________	______________

B IN PAIRS At random, choose one thing from List A and one thing from List B. How are those two things the same? Discuss and make a list of as many ways as you can.

A: We've got a cell phone and a guitar. They can both play music. Anything else?

B: You use both of them with your fingers!

CONFIDENT COMMUNICATOR
KEEP TALKING

To ask for further suggestions, use the following expressions:
What else do they have in common?
Are there any other ways that they're the same?
What other ideas do you have?

Language and Life

Design Thinking – An App

A 3.06 **Read the article. Then answer the questions.**

The Trouble With Social Media

Social media companies have been feeling worried recently. People have realized that there are a few problems connected to social media. One is the problem of confirmation bias. Our online friends make comments and share posts that we already agree with. We accept them as true and we never see any evidence of other opinions. This can mean that we share and like false stories more easily because they match what we already believe.

There are other problems, too. Some people spend too much time on social media. They update their status many times a day and their phones show notifications of other people's posts. This often means they waste time, or they ignore their real-life family and friends. They might also become anxious about how many shares or likes their posts get. Other people experience cyberbullying, where people make up comments about them. That can have an effect on people's lives and their health.

Another issue is our digital footprint. Every time we post, share, or comment, we leave a digital record. It often follows us for a very long time. When you apply for a job or when you meet someone new, they might check your social media. What will they see? Are you sure that you want them to see everything you've posted?

Finally, people share a lot of information on social media. They share their location, when they're on vacation, and what they do every day. That can leave the person vulnerable to crime or other problems.

Many people agree that we need to find ways to help people be safer on social media and to think more about the information they see and share.

1 What five problems with social media are mentioned? ______

______

2 Have you or anyone you know ever had those problems with social media? ______

B **You work for a company. Read the email from your manager. What does she want you to do?**

New Message

Subject: app idea

Hi all,

We see a gap in the market for an app to help people deal with problems created by social media. It might fact-check stories in the media. Or it might help delete your social footprint. It could be anything, really. See if you can come up with a few ideas and we'll meet to discuss them.

Regards,

Rose

Send

C **On your own, think of an app to suggest to your manager. Make a short note of what your app does.**

an app that immediately checks the facts in any story you see online

My suggested app: ______________________________

D IN GROUPS **You are going to use a method called starbursting. Read the description. Have you used starbursting or a similar technique before?**

Starbursting is a way of brainstorming good questions to ask about a suggestion. In the middle of a star, you write the suggestion. On the points of the star are the words *What, Who, Where, When, How,* and *Why*. You use these to come up with questions to ask about the suggestion. For example, you might ask: "Who will use this app?" By asking and answering the questions, you provide more detail on the suggestion and highlight key considerations.

E IN GROUPS **Write your app from C in the middle of the star. Use the starbursting method to write questions to ask about the app. Then ask and answer the questions for each person's app.**

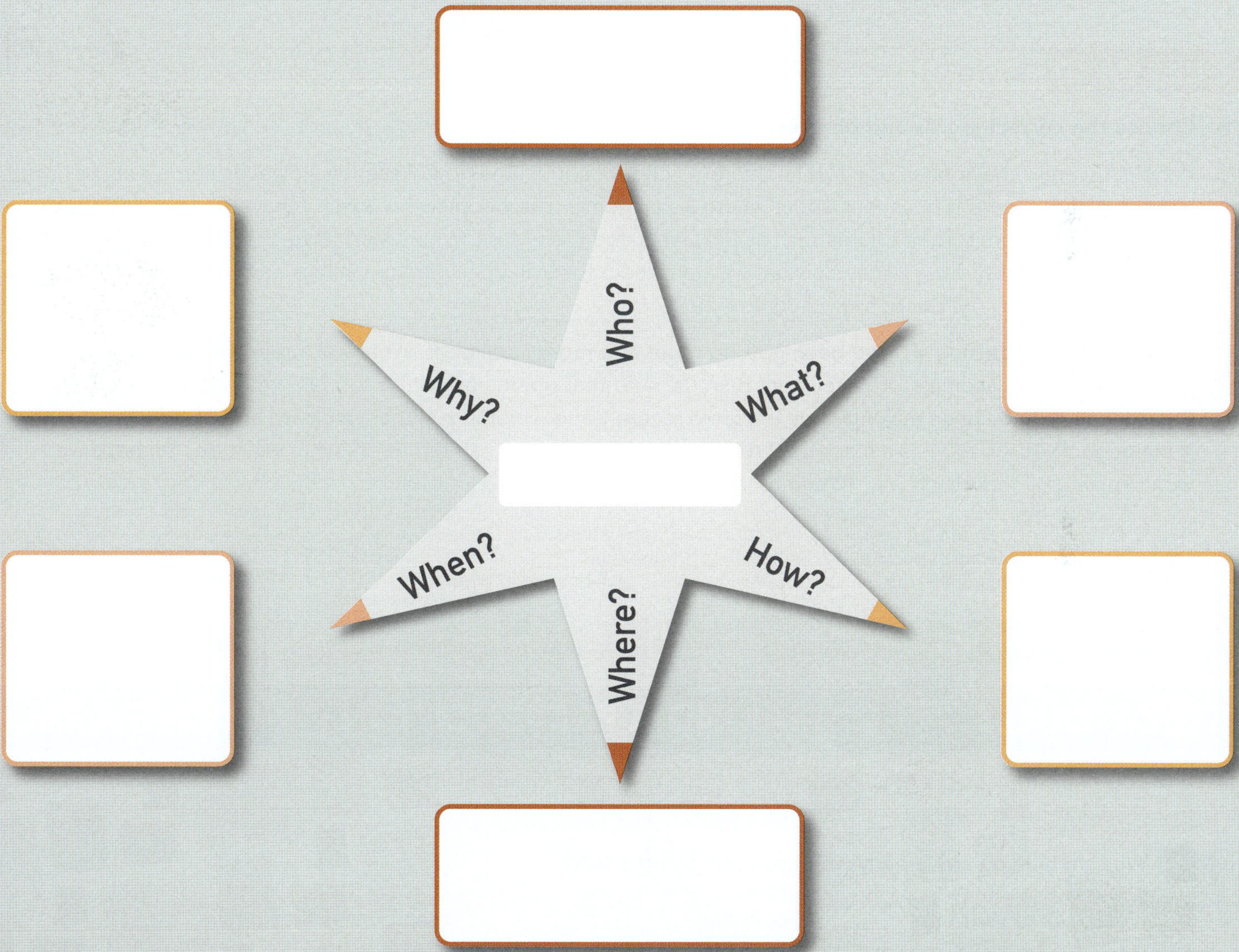

F **Compare the different apps from each group and choose which you like the best. Tell the class about the apps and about the answers to the questions in E.**

G **Discuss the questions.**

1 How useful did you find the starbursting method?
2 What key issues did the process highlight?
3 In what other situations do you think starbursting would help?

MAKE IT DIGITAL

Research the most popular apps in your country on different online app sites. Why do you think they are popular?

VOCABULARY review

SCORE: / 10

A Complete the sentences.

1. I'll create a fantastic design for your website. You can rely ______________ me!
2. I wonder how great writers make ______________ such wonderful stories.
3. I find it hard to concentrate ______________ my work with all this noise!
4. When did you take ______________ running in your spare time?
5. You'll remember more if you pay attention ______________ what the speaker is saying.

B Complete the sentences using forms of the words in parentheses.

1. After brainstorming ideas, we finally found a ______________ (solve) to the problem.
2. Many people have lost their jobs recently and ______________ (employ) is a big problem.
3. It takes a lot of ______________ (create) to produce beautiful works of art.
4. Do you think AI will be ______________ (danger) in the future?
5. Computers are becoming more and more ______________ (power) every year.

GRAMMAR review

SCORE: / 10

A Choose the correct words and phrases.

People **1 were / have been** using AI in different ways for some time now. Recently, however, some people have been **2 raised / raising** questions about where it's all going. The people who **3 will / have been** asking these questions include important figures such as Bill Gates and Elon Musk. When we **4 have / will have** machines that can think for themselves, will they do what we want them to? Will intelligent machines learn right from wrong before we **5 learn / will learn** how to control them?

Machines **6 have getting / have been getting** more and more intelligent. What will happen when our machines **7 become / will become** more intelligent than us? And that point may not be too far in the future. Researchers **8 has made / have been making** huge progress recently in developing AI that can learn and can design the next generation of AI. As soon as a machine **9 realizes / will realize** we can turn it off, what will it do? Perhaps we won't know until that day finally **10 comes / will come**.

16–20 correct: You can use phrasal verbs and form word derivatives. You can use future time clauses and the present perfect progressive.
0–15 correct: Look again at the Vocabulary and Grammar sections in the unit.

TOTAL SCORE: / 20

WHAT DO YOU KNOW NOW? Look back at page 27 and add the words you know now to the box.

STUDY SKILLS MAKING A PRESENTATION OR GIVING A TALK

Take the quiz about making a presentation or giving a talk. Go to **Study Skills** on page 129 to find the answers. Then learn more about the topic.

1 Why should you arrive early when you are giving a talk?
a to make last-minute changes to your talk
b to have time for tea or coffee
c to meet the audience members as they arrive

2 When you are giving a talk, where should you look?
a at one person in the audience
b into the eyes of a few different people
c at your notes

3 It's best if your slides don't contain a lot of text.
a True
b False

4 What should you wear when you are giving a talk?
a professional-looking clothing that you have worn before
b comfortable old clothing that you would wear to relax in
c fashionable new clothing that you would wear to a special event

UNIT 4

Beyond Words

WHAT DO YOU ALREADY KNOW?

1 Think about words you know about communication. Write the words.

2 IN PAIRS Share and compare your ideas. Add more words to your lists.

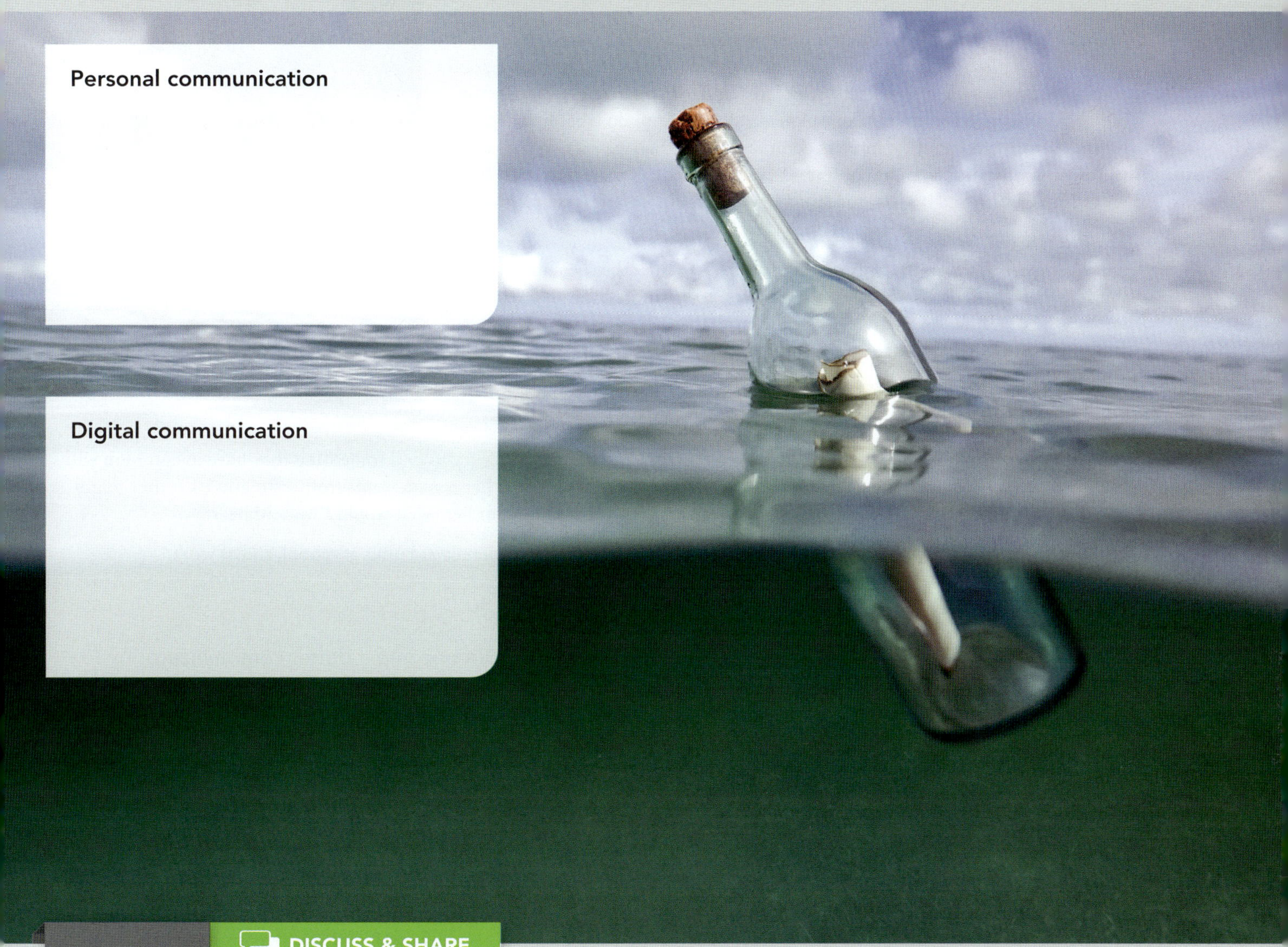

Personal communication

Digital communication

VIDEO

DISCUSS & SHARE

3 IN GROUPS Watch the video and answer the question.

SYM Would you rather call someone or text them?

In this unit, you will ...

- present a subject you know, ask questions and assess someone's body language, and decide on the best means of communication for different situations.
- use thinking skills: evaluate, apply, and predict.
- read about how to be a good communicator.
- learn strategies to use eye contact, use language to ask for more information, and to make your meaning clearer.
- use reasoning skills to discuss the pros and cons of a company proposal.
- follow a PR professional to learn about this job and the skills needed for this industry.

READING

A **Do you think you are a good communicator? Why or why not?**

B 4.01 READING SKILL—Read for gist **Read the article quickly. Then choose the best summary.**

Being a Good Communicator

Many of us find it hard to communicate. You may know what you want to say but not know how. What makes a good communicator? You might think a good communicator is someone who can speak well and explain his or her ideas. You might think a good communicator can **persuade** people to do what he or she wants. However, there's a lot more to communication than expressing yourself well. Communication is an important skill in our personal, academic, and professional lives. And it's easy to learn a few simple communication techniques.

The first is active listening. Good communicators listen carefully to understand the other person's thoughts. They repeat ideas back to the other person to show they understand. They also encourage the person to say more by asking relevant questions. For example, a good communicator might say: "I hear you saying that you're unhappy with your major. How, exactly?"

Good communicators are **honest**. In an argument with a friend, you don't help communication when you pretend that everything is fine. Good communicators talk honestly about how they feel.

Finally, good communicators make a personal **connection** with people. They try to find something they **have in common** with the person they are speaking to. That helps them to understand what the other person wants from a situation. Or they might try to put themselves in the other person's position and ask: "If I were him or her, what would I want to hear?"

Using these techniques will help to improve your relationships with other people at home, at school, and at work.

1 Communication is a way of getting other people to agree with you. You do this by asking them questions and talking about your feelings.

2 You can become a better communicator by listening carefully, telling the truth, and building relationships with people.

C **Read the article in B again and choose the correct options.**

1 What point is the writer making in the first paragraph?
   - **a** It isn't right to try to change other people's opinions.
   - **b** Communication isn't just about explaining things well.

2 According to the writer, active listening is a way of …
   - **a** understanding someone's opinion.
   - **b** getting people to understand you.

3 According to the writer, good communicators …
   - **a** pretend they feel the same way as the other person.
   - **b** tell the truth about their emotions.

4 It can help you understand what people want when you …
   - **a** look for things that are true for both of you.
   - **b** help them understand a situation correctly.

D THINKING SKILL—Evaluate **Decide what other things make someone a good communicator.**

VOCABULARY

A **Complete the sentences using the words in bold in READING B.**

1 You need to explain your ideas clearly to ____________ other people to do what you want.
2 I find it easy to communicate with you because we ____________ a lot ____________.
3 I have a very strong ____________ with my twin brother and I know what he's thinking.
4 Be ____________. You don't like my new hairstyle, do you?

GRAMMAR infinitives with *to*

A Match the sentences (1–4) to the correct explanations (a–d).

1 Many of us find it hard to communicate. ______
2 You may know what you want to say but not know how. ______
3 You might think a good communicator can persuade people to do what he or she wants. ______
4 ... listen carefully to understand the other person's thoughts. ______

We use the infinitive with *to* ...
a to express a purpose
b after some verbs (*advise, tell, warn, persuade*, etc.) + direct object
c after some verbs (*agree, like, prefer, want*, etc.)
d after some adjectives (*easy, happy, hard, ready*, etc.)

For more practice, go to page 146.

B Circle one more example of each use in READING B.

1 to express a purpose
2 after a verb + direct object
3 after a verb
4 after an adjective

C Complete the sentences with the correct forms of the words from the box.

agree	appear	communicate	learn
make	see	understand	

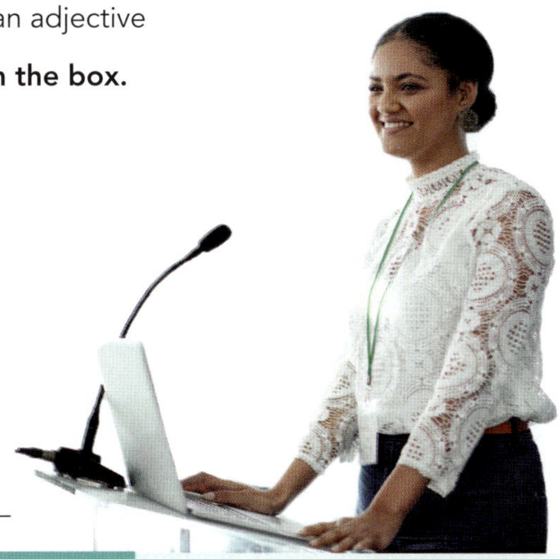

Good Public Speakers
All public speakers try **1** ______________ their message to their audience. Good ones plan their presentation carefully **2** ______________ sure their message is clear. They know that it's hard **3** ______________ a complicated speech, so they make it as simple as they can. Then, they start **4** ______________ the material. Many practice in front of a mirror **5** ______________ how confident they appear. Appearing confident is very important in getting your audience **6** ______________ with your ideas. Everyone gets nervous, but successful speakers try not **7** ______________ nervous to the audience.

MAKE IT DIGITAL

People in many careers need to give presentations. Watch expert presenters online and learn from them. Look for opportunities to give short presentations in class.

D IN PAIRS Have you ever given a presentation?

SPEAKING

A Think of a subject you know something about. It could be an academic subject, a famous person, a kind of music, etc. Make notes for a short presentation to a small group.

Subject: ______________________________
Main points: ______________________________
____

B IN GROUPS Take turns giving a short presentation (2–3 minutes) on your chosen subject. Use the Confident Communicator box to help you.

CONFIDENT COMMUNICATOR
KEEP TALKING

To be a good communicator, make eye contact with the person or people you are talking to. When you are talking to a group of people, try to make eye contact with each of them equally.

VOCABULARY ways to communicate

A Complete the sentences with words from the box.

distance	position	speed	touch
tone	space	volume	

1 Your ______________ of voice is the way you say something and it shows how you feel.
2 Some people talk at a fast ______________, which can be hard to understand.
3 How much personal ______________ do you need when you are talking to someone?
4 The ______________ of your voice is how loud or quiet it is.
5 The ______________ from New York to London is 5,567 kilometers.
6 The ______________ of your arms can mean you are friendly or it can mean you feel uncomfortable.
7 In some countries, ______________ is a part of communication and people often put their hands on each other's arms.

B IN PAIRS Think about your country compared to other countries. Choose and then talk about your choices with a partner.

	Strongly agree	Agree	Neither agree nor disagree	Disagree	Strongly disagree
1 People talk at high speed and high volume.	☐	☐	☐	☐	☐
2 People need a lot of personal space.	☐	☐	☐	☐	☐
3 Touch is a part of communication.	☐	☐	☐	☐	☐

LISTENING

A Look at the picture. What do you think they are talking about? What does their body language tell you?

B 4.02 LISTENING SKILL—Listen for specific information Listen to Part 1 of an interview and label the diagram and key.

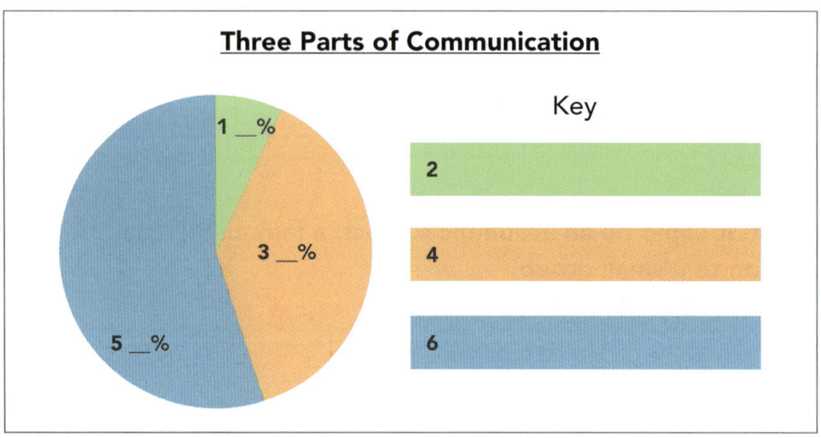

C 4.03 Read the sentences and predict what the missing words or short phrases could be. Then listen to Part 2 and complete the sentences.

1 It's easy to misunderstand when communicating ______________ because there's no tone of voice.
2 People in Romania want almost twice as much personal space as people in ______________.
3 We often have our arms ______________ when we are interested in another person's opinion.
4 You need to be careful when someone's body language means ______________ of their words.

GLOSSARY

verbal (adj): connected to words

D **THINKING SKILLS—Apply** **How close you would stand to (a) a stranger, (b) someone you know, and (c) a close friend? Record your answer on the diagram and compare with a partner.**

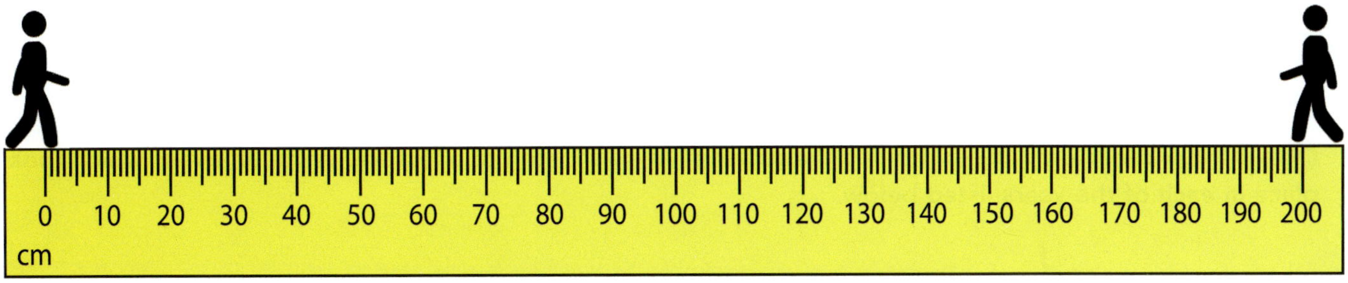

GRAMMAR separable and non-separable phrasal verbs

A **Check (✓) the correct sentences.**

1
- ☐ I **looked up** "body language" online.
- ☐ I **looked** "body language" **up** online.
- ☐ I **looked** it **up** online.
- ☐ I **looked up** it online.

2
- ☐ You can **rely on** Ruby to give a good talk.
- ☐ You can **rely** Ruby **on** to give a good talk.
- ☐ You can **rely on** her to give a good talk.
- ☐ You can **rely** her **on** to give a good talk.

B **Choose the correct options.**

With separable phrasal verbs, you **1 can / can't** put a noun between the verb and the particle. With non-separable phrasal verbs, you **2 can / can't**. With separable phrasal verbs, we **3 always / never** separate the verb and the particle when the object is a pronoun (*you*, *it*, *them*, etc.). Phrasal verbs with a particle plus a preposition (e.g., *come up with*) are **4 always / never** separable.

For more practice, go to page 147.

C **Choose the correct options. Both may be correct.**

1. Her body language told me she was **making the story up / making up the story**.
2. Her body language told me she was **making it up / making up it**.
3. I told Matt you would **call back him / call him back**.
4. You should **take up psychology / take psychology up** to learn more about body language.
5. I **ran into Alice / ran Alice into** outside class yesterday and we had a good chat.

D **IN PAIRS** **Do you know when someone is making a story up? Discuss.**

SPEAKING

A **Write three statements about yourself. Two of the statements should be true and one should be false. Don't tell anyone which one is false.**

I once went to New York. I'm thinking of taking the violin up. I have a cat named Dog.

B **IN PAIRS** **Follow the instructions. Use the Confident Communicator box to help you.**

Find someone in class who doesn't know you very well. Ask each other questions about your statements. As your partner talks, watch his or her body language carefully. Can you tell which statement is false?

CONFIDENT COMMUNICATOR
KEEP TALKING

To ask someone to provide more information, use the following phrases:
Tell me more about *taking up the violin.*
What happened when *you went to New York?*
What else can you tell me about *your cat?*

LISTENING

A Discuss how communication has changed in your lifetime.

B 4.04 LISTENING SKILL—Listen for the order of events **Listen to a lecture. Write an event which took place in each of the years listed below.**

1971	1973	1992	1999	2007	2009	2011
________	________	________	________	________	________	________

C 4.04 **Listen again and answer the questions.**

1. How many emails are sent each day? ____________________
2. What percentage of people have a cell phone? ____________________
3. How many emojis are there today? ____________________
4. How many apps are there for the iPhone? ____________________
5. How many messages are sent through WhatsApp each day? ____________________
6. How many people use Snapchat? ____________________

D THINKING SKILL—Predict **Calculate how many messages of different kinds (emails, text messages, etc.) you send each year. Compare with a partner.**

PRONUNCIATION electronic communication

A 4.05 **How do you say each of the phrases in italics? Discuss with a partner. Then listen and check.**

Go to *www.macmillan.com*
My email is *lisa_jackson3@emailtoday.org*
Under the picture, it says *#selfie* and *#mybestlook*
My email is *carrie-smith@fly.org*

MAKE IT YOURS

Think about other types of electronic communication you use. How do you say the phrases associated with those types of communication?

B **Practice saying the sentences in A.**

VOCABULARY emojis

A **Write a word or phrase from the box under each emoji.**

clap	point	punch	shake hands	smile	thumbs up	wave

1 ____________

2 ____________

3 ____________

4 ____________

5 ____________

6 ____________

7 ____________

B IN PAIRS **Do you use emojis? Why or why not? Discuss.**

WRITING text message and email

A Read the text message. Match each informal phrase (1–8) with a more formal phrase (a–h).

[1] Hi Pedro. [2] Come to my party next Friday. [3] It's at the Sunrise Café, 7pm. [4] It's for my 21st birthday. 👍🎉🎂 [5] Hope you can be there. [6] Don't worry about a present. 😀 [7] Can you come? [8] ♥ Alexa

1 ______	**5** ______
2 ______	**6** ______
3 ______	**7** ______
4 ______	**8** ______

a The party is taking place at the Sunrise Café at 7 p.m.
b Please let me know if you are able to attend.
c I would like to invite you to my party next Friday.
d The event is to celebrate my 21st birthday.
e Best wishes,
f I hope you will be able to come.
g Dear Pedro,
h Please don't feel you need to bring a gift.

B Read the email and underline two sentences that are informal. Rewrite the sentences more formally.

New Message

Dear Amelie,

Come to my house-warming party. I have just moved into a new apartment and I thought it would be a good chance to get to know everyone in the office. The party is taking place on the 15th after work. I hope you will be able to come. Don't bring any gifts.

Please let me know if you are able to come so that I know how many people to expect.

Sincerely,
Millie

Send

1 ______________________________
2 ______________________________

C Read the information. Then write an email to a colleague you don't know very well inviting him or her to the event.

Event: a party to celebrate my birthday
Time and place: my home, 4th, 8:30 p.m.
Comments: no gifts, I need to know who's coming

D Swap emails with a partner. Check for the correct spelling and punctuation and the right level of formality.

SPEAKING

A Which is the best way to communicate in each situation?

	Text message	Email	Phone call
1 telling a friend some bad news	☐	☐	☐
2 congratulating a friend on success	☐	☐	☐
3 wishing your grandparents a happy anniversary	☐	☐	☐

B IN PAIRS Why would you use different means of communication in different situations? Discuss.

CONFIDENT COMMUNICATOR
KEEP TALKING

To make your meaning clearer, use the following phrases:
I mean, *you can't give someone bad news in a text message.*
In other words, *you need to speak to someone in person when it's serious.*

Language and Life

Reason Effectively – An International Company

A 4.06 **Read the article. Then answer the questions.**

Communication Problems

Businesses and other organizations succeed when the people communicate well with each other. There needs to be a free flow of information and instructions. Unfortunately, communication often goes wrong.

One reason for communication problems is that in large, multinational corporations, people often come from different cultures and speak different languages. They may use a common language to communicate, often English, but that doesn't remove the possibility of misunderstandings. People from some cultures, such as the US and Western Europe, may think it's important to clearly express their ideas and say how they feel. They might not see a problem in correcting a colleague or criticizing an idea. However, this can make people from some *other* cultures feel very uncomfortable. Similar problems can happen when people are from the same culture but have different life experiences.

Another reason for problems is communication technology. Many of us work from home at least some of the time these days. We communicate with colleagues through software such as Skype or Google Hangouts, and it doesn't always work perfectly. When we don't completely understand something and we are not able to check our understanding, it can lead to problems.

You might be surprised to hear that another possible reason for communication problems is friendships at work. Normally, we think of friends as people we communicate well with. However, mixing personal and professional communication isn't a good idea. It makes some people feel uncomfortable and it can start arguments.

Many organizations work hard to improve communication, for example, organizing diversity training sessions for employees. Another idea is a no-email day. One day a week, no one sends emails. Instead, they speak to people on the phone or meet in person. Small changes like that can make a big difference.

1 Why might there be misunderstandings in a multinational corporation?

2 Why can there be misunderstandings between people from the same culture?

3 How can communication technology cause communication problems?

4 Why does the writer say "You might be surprised"?

5 What happens on a no-email day?

6 What difference do you think a no-email day has on the people in a company?

B Read and evaluate the information. Think about what you need to do. What are your next steps?

You work for a large corporation with offices in different countries. Managers have noticed some communication problems recently. They feel that people from different countries seem to misunderstand each other, although they all speak English well. They are looking for ideas to improve everyone's communication skills and they have asked you and your team for suggestions.

C IN GROUPS Analyze each of the ideas and identify the pros and cons. Add more ideas of your own. Use the phrases to discuss your thoughts.

One good thing about diversity training is …

Overseas visits are useful because …

One problem with language training is ….

1. Diversity training

Advantages: ______________________________

Disadvantages: ______________________________

2. Overseas visits

Advantages: ______________________________

Disadvantages: ______________________________

3. Language training

Advantages: ______________________________

Disadvantages: ______________________________

4. Other idea

____

____

D Decide which ideas you are going to suggest. Choose one or two.

E Tell the class which ideas you have chosen. Explain how you made your choice.

F Discuss the questions.

1 What reasoning skills did you use to form an opinion and select an idea?

2 In what other situations do you think this process would be useful?

MAKE IT DIGITAL

Go to your college or company's website. Do they have a diversity and inclusion policy? Do they offer any training for this?

VOCABULARY review

SCORE: / 10

A Complete the sentences with words from the box.

common connection	express persuade	shake smile	thumbs tone	volume wave

All human cultures have at least two things in **1** __________. First of all, we all use language to **2** __________ ourselves. Exactly how we speak may change. We may speak at a higher **3** __________ when we are excited or use a different **4** __________ of voice when we are angry. We may speak in a certain way when we want to **5** __________ somebody to do something. But all of us use words to try to make a **6** __________ to other people every day. Second, we all communicate non-verbally through gestures. Interestingly, a **7** __________ up gesture generally means something good in Western countries, but it isn't a polite gesture in West Africa. People in many countries **8** __________ hands when they meet, but the strength used might be different. And in some countries people just **9** __________ at each other to say hello. There are even differences in how often people **10** __________ to show they are happy!

GRAMMAR review

SCORE: / 10

A Use the prompts to write sentences in your notebook.

1 It is hard / persuade people / do / what you want them / do.
2 It's important / try / relax / if you want your audience / agree with you.
3 I always advise public speakers / not speak too fast.
4 Speak to people in person / avoid communication problems and / see their body language.
5 I prefer / speak to small groups because it's possible / see if they're listening.

B Check (✓) the correct responses. Rewrite the incorrect responses in your notebook.

1 "When did you take up karate?" ☐ "I took it up about a year ago."
2 "How did you come up with the idea for your app?" ☐ "I came it up with when I was at work."
3 "Is your story based on real life?" ☐ "No. I just made up it."
4 "Do you use your smartphone every day?" ☐ "Oh, yes! I rely it on for everything!"
5 "What does *irrelevant* mean?" ☐ "Why don't you look up it in the dictionary?"

16–20 correct: You can talk about communication and gestures. You can use infinitives with *to* and separable and non-separable phrasal verbs.
0–15 correct: Look again at the Vocabulary and Grammar sections in the unit.

TOTAL SCORE: / 20

WHAT DO YOU KNOW NOW? Look back at page 37 and add the words you know now to the boxes.

FOLLOW A PRO COMMUNICATION

Take the quiz about communication. Go to **Follow A Pro** on page 130 to find the answers. Then learn more about working in communication.

1 Where do companies spend the most money on advertising?
a television **b** newspapers **c** the internet

2 What percentage of the world's population can access the internet?
a 30%–35% **b** 55%–60% **c** 85%–90%

3 When was writing invented?
a 3,000 BCE **b** 500 BCE **c** 500 CE

4 When was the first radio program broadcast?
a 1906 **b** 1922 **c** 1935

UNIT 5

One Planet

WHAT DO YOU ALREADY KNOW?

1 Think about the words you know for weather. Write the words.

2 **IN PAIRS** Share and compare your ideas. Add more words to your lists.

Weather

Severe weather

VIDEO

DISCUSS & SHARE

3 **IN GROUPS** **Watch the video and answer the question.**

SYM Do you think the changes in severe weather are natural or caused by people?

In this unit, you will ...

- discuss global warming problems, talk about solutions, and brainstorm products.
- use thinking skills: summarize, analyze, and categorize.
- read about climate change.
- use strategies to start speaking for a group, talk about problems and solutions, and comment on ideas.
- use global-competence skills to explain your ideas about environmental projects.
- learn strategies to improve reading speed.

Climate Change

VOCABULARY

A Match the words in the box with the definitions.

climate degree forest fire melt trap weather

1 ______________________: a unit to measure temperature
2 ______________________: to keep something like air or gas in one place
3 ______________________: conditions in the atmosphere like temperature, rain, clouds, etc.
4 ______________________: a large area of trees burning
5 ______________________: the type of weather that a country or region has
6 ______________________: to change a solid material to a liquid

MAKE IT YOURS

Do these words used to describe climate change describe the changes where you live?

B IN PAIRS Test your partner. Take turns reading definitions from A and saying the correct word.

READING

A 5.01 IN PAIRS Choose *True* or *False*. Then read the article to check your answers.

1 Global warming and climate change are the same thing. True / False
2 Global warming is caused by the greenhouse effect. True / False
3 If the Earth's temperature rises just a little, there won't be any problems. True / False
4 If the polar ice caps melt, the seas will rise. True / False
5 If we do nothing, some coastal cities may disappear. True / False

FAQs About Climate Change

Followers

1 Are climate change and global warming the same thing?
Global warming refers to the general rise in the Earth's temperatures that has happened since the beginning of the Industrial Revolution. Climate change refers to all of the changes in weather and climate that are caused by global warming, such as hotter summers, more severe storms, and more forest fires.

2 What causes global warming?
Global warming began with the Industrial Revolution when we started using fossil fuels—carbon-based fuels like oil and gas—but most global warming has happened since the 1970s. When we burn fossil fuels, they produce carbon dioxide. The carbon dioxide in the atmosphere traps heat and holds it near the Earth. Other types of gases, like methane, also trap heat near the Earth. This is called the greenhouse effect.

3 Does it really matter if the Earth is only a few degrees warmer than it was?
It is true that the Earth is only about 0.99°C warmer than it was in the mid-20th century, but if temperatures go up even a small amount, big changes take place. Sea levels rise and more severe weather events happen. The United Nations predicts that if temperatures rise more than 1.5°C, the effect on our lives will be extreme. If we didn't burn so many fossil fuels, the effects of global warming wouldn't be so serious.

4 What are the effects of global warming and climate change?
Unless we stop global warming, the polar ice caps will melt and sea levels will rise. This will affect Arctic and Antarctic species like polar bears and penguins, and it will mean more floods in coastal cities. Some areas will have hotter summers with long droughts and terrible fires. Other areas will have colder winters with bad ice and snowstorms. There will be more severe weather events like tornadoes and hurricanes.

If we don't do anything about global warming, there will be terrible consequences. Some coastal cities like Miami, Osaka, and parts of Rio de Janeiro may disappear. Many species of animals may also disappear, and this will change the Earth's ecosystems. One thing is certain: our planet will not be the same place it is today.

GLOSSARY

drought (n): a long period of time when there is little or no rain and plants die

B **READING SKILL—Identify explanations, definitions, and examples** Find and underline the following things in the text in A.

1 definitions of global warming and climate change (Question 1)
2 three examples of changes caused by global warming (Question 1)
3 an explanation of what fossil fuels are (Question 2)
4 an explanation of what the greenhouse effect is (Question 2)
5 two examples of severe weather events (Question 4)

C **THINKING SKILL—Summarize** Explain why scientists say that today's climate change and global warming are primarily caused by human activity.

GRAMMAR review of conditionals

A **Match the conditionals (1–3) to the verb forms (a–c) to complete the rules.**

If temperatures go up even a small amount, big changes take place.
If that happens, the effect on our lives will be extreme.
Unless we stop global warming, the polar ice caps will melt.
If we didn't burn so many fossil fuels, global warming wouldn't happen so quickly.

1 (zero conditional) *If/Unless* + simple present verb, ______
2 (first conditional) *If/Unless* + simple present verb, ______
3 (second conditional) *If/Unless* + simple past verb, ______

a + *will/won't* + base verb
b + *would/wouldn't* + base verb
c + simple present verb

For more practice, go to page 148.

B **Label the sentences *zero*, *first*, or *second* according to the rules in A.**

1 If we stopped using fossil fuels, there would be less carbon dioxide. ______________
2 If sea levels rise, some cities will be in danger. ______________
3 Ice melts if the temperature goes above 0°C. ______________
4 If you watch a program about global warming, how do you feel? ______________
5 If you buy a new car, will you buy an electric one? ______________
6 If you could change one thing in your town or city, what would it be? ______________

C **IN PAIRS** **Discuss questions 4, 5, and 6 in B.**

SPEAKING

A **IN PAIRS** **Discuss which of the effects of global warming are affecting your country. Make some suggestions about what will happen and possible solutions. Make notes in your notebooks.**

- Rising sea levels
- Drought
- Severe rainstorms
- Hurricanes
- Tornadoes
- Severe winters

If sea levels continue to rise, we will probably lose three of our major coastal cities.

There are already more droughts in the center of the country, and they will get worse. This will affect our food supply because ...

If we changed to electric cars, we would produce less pollution.

B **IN GROUPS** **Work with another pair. Compare your ideas from A. Do you all agree? Use the Confident Communicator box to help you.**

A: We think that if sea levels rise, we'll lose ..., ..., and ... .
B: We agree about ... and ... . We might not lose ... because it's higher.

CONFIDENT COMMUNICATOR
START TALKING

To start the conversation when speaking for a group, use the following phrases:
We think ... / We believe ... / As we understand it, ... / As far as we know, ... / Our view is ... / We decided ...

VOCABULARY taking action

A Complete the sentences with words and phrases from the box.

create laws	pay a fine	reduce
don't allow	provide	require

Air and water pollution: Make companies that produce pollution **1** ____________.
Have lower taxes for people and companies that use clean energy.
Trash: **2** ____________ free recycling services. **3** ____________ the use of plastic.
Make people pay for plastic bags in stores and grocery stores. Make products that **4** ____________ less packaging.
Overfishing: Limit fishing of certain types of fish. **5** ____________ certain types of fishing nets.
Endangered species: **6** ____________ to protect species that are disappearing.

PRONUNCIATION word stress in verb phrases

A 5.02 Listen to the phrases and underline the stressed word in each phrase. What type of word is stressed?

verb + noun

1. reduce pollution
2. provide recycling
3. create laws

verb + adjective/adverb + noun

4. pay for plastic bags
5. require less packaging
6. use clean energy

B IN PAIRS Practice reading the sentences with stress on the correct words.

1. They should create a law that requires less packaging.
2. The city should provide recycling and support businesses that use clean energy.

LISTENING

A Discuss the questions as a class.

Do you think young people in your country are very concerned about environmental problems? Why or why not?

B 5.03 LISTENING SKILL—Listen for main ideas Listen to four short radio interviews. Which four environmental problems do the speakers talk about?

C 5.03 Choose the correct options. Then listen again and check.

1. The first person thinks the main cause of global warming is companies using …
   a fossil fuels. **b** taxes. **c** clean energy.
2. According to the second person, … of the people in the world don't have clean water to drink.
   a thousands **b** millions **c** billions
3. The third speaker is worried about trash, especially …
   a glass. **b** plastic. **c** metal.
4. The fourth speaker says that overfishing could destroy her country's …
   a oceans. **b** ecosystems. **c** economy.
5. The host says that he hopes … are taking environmental problems seriously.
   a governments **b** all countries **c** young people

D IN GROUPS THINKING SKILL—Analyze Prioritize the environmental issues mentioned in B. Which two are the most important?

GRAMMAR present and future hopes and wishes

A Write whether the sentences refer to the present (*P*) or the future (*F*).

1 I hope our generation is taking environmental problems seriously. ____
2 I hope our generation makes a lot of changes to help save the planet! ____
3 I hope all cities will provide free recycling soon. ____
4 I wish fossil fuels didn't exist! ____
5 I wish every country had stronger laws against water pollution. ____
6 I wish my government would make fishing companies reduce certain types of fishing. ____

B Match the structures (1–4) with the functions (a–d).

1 *wish* + *would* or *could* ____
2 *hope* + simple present, present progressive, or *can* ____
3 *hope* + *will*, *can*, or simple present ____
4 *wish* + simple past ____

a something that you want and expect to be true in the present
b something that you want and expect to happen in the future
c something that you would like to be true in the present but isn't
d something that you would like to happen in the future but probably won't

For more practice, go to page 148.

C Complete the conversations with the correct forms of the words in parentheses.

A: I hope it **1** ____________ (not rain) this weekend!
B: Let's see … My phone says it will be clear on the weekend. I hope that it **2** ____________ (be) correct!
A: I wish I **3** ____________ (have) more time to do volunteer work.
B: Me, too. I hope I **4** ____________ (can) do some volunteer work next semester.
A: I wish my brother **5** ____________ (help) me with my ecology project, but he says he can't.
B: I wish I **6** ____________ (not have) so much work because I would help you with it.
A: I hope the government **7** ____________ (create) a new soda tax law.
B: Yeah. I wish they **8** ____________ (create) a tax on plastic bottles, too!

D IN PAIRS Change the underlined information in C to make new conversations with your own ideas.

SPEAKING

A Think about the answers to these questions. Make notes.

1 Which environmental issues are most important in your country? Why?
2 What do you wish your country would do about these issues?
3 What do you hope your generation will do about environmental problems in the future?

A: I think global warming is the most important issue for us because we have two coasts.
B: I agree. If the seas rise, we'll lose some of our cities, and also, we'll have a lot of hurricanes and other bad storms. I wish we had stronger air pollution laws.
C: I hope young people will help educate the public about the problem of global warming.

B IN GROUPS Discuss your answers to the questions in A. Do most of you have similar ideas? Use the Confident Communicator box to help you.

CONFIDENT COMMUNICATOR
KEEP TALKING

To talk about problems and solutions, use the following phrases:
Problems
One problem/issue is …
The biggest/main problem/issue is…
… is a big/major/serious problem.
Solutions
If we had stronger laws, we wouldn't have so much pollution.
What if we had stronger pollution laws?
I think we need / should have stronger pollution laws.

Hope for the Future

LISTENING

A Match the environmental solutions (1–8) with the photos (a–h).

a

______

b

______

c

______

d

______

e

______

f

______

g

______

h

______

1 plant pots made from tires ______
2 recycled paper flip-flops ______
3 super trees ______
4 recycled plastic houses ______
5 fog catchers ______
6 school desks made from recycled materials ______
7 living walls ______
8 green roofs ______

B 5.04 **LISTENING SKILL—Listen for details** **Listen to a class discussion. Under the photos a–h in A, write the name of the country where each environmental solution is taking place.**

C 5.04 **THINKING SKILL—Categorize** **Listen again and decide who should do each of the eight projects. Categorize the projects as *private companies, the government,* or *either*. Give reasons for your opinions.**

I think the government would have to … because it would be very expensive.

MAKE IT REAL

Informal ways to say strange or unusual: *weird, bizarre, wild*

VOCABULARY materials and products

A Match the descriptions with words from the box.

coconut	flip-flop	net	pot	roof	rubber	steel	tire

1 a material with spaces made of string, rope, or metal wire: ______
2 the part of a wheel that is filled with air: ______
3 a container used to cook or to plant flowers or other plants: ______
4 the fruit of a kind of palm tree: ______
5 a strong metal made of iron and carbon: ______
6 the top of a house or other building: ______
7 a type of sandal with a V-shaped strap: ______
8 a flexible material similar to plastic that comes from a tree: ______

B IN PAIRS Think of other things that can be made from recycled materials. Discuss.

WRITING

A **Read the essay. Does the writer have a generally positive or generally negative opinion of his country's actions on the environment? Tell a partner.**

My country has changed a lot since I was a small child. Twenty years ago, air pollution was terrible in big cities, and water pollution was very bad, too. The government has given tax breaks to industries that moved to new locations, and they have created strong anti-pollution laws. Companies that pollute the air or water have to pay big fines. My city has built new parks and other green spaces, and it has created new pollution laws for vehicles.

The results from the changes have been positive, but I wish we would do more to help with problems like deforestation and global warming. If universities offered programs to train people in rural areas to do different jobs, they wouldn't have to cut down trees to get money. Also, my city gives people free trees to plant in their yards. There will be a lot more trees if all of the cities do that. Another thing that helps with the problem of air pollution and global warming in general is roof gardens. If companies put gardens on their roofs, the plants would put oxygen into the air and take out carbon dioxide. I believe that my country is doing some good things for the environment, and I hope we will do many more things in the near future.

B **IN PAIRS Find and underline actions and their results in the second paragraph of the text in A. Say which is the action and which is the result in each case.**

If universities offered programs to train people in rural areas to do different jobs (action), they wouldn't have to cut down trees to get money (result).

C **Think about environmental projects in your country. Make a list of actions your government or companies have taken and the results for the environment. Make another list of actions you recommend and the results.**

Action	*Result*
Reduced taxes for companies that move to new locations	*Less air pollution in big cities*
Recommended action	*Result*
Plant more trees in the cities	*More oxygen in the air*

D **Use your notes from C to write a short essay similar to the one in A.**

SPEAKING

A **IN PAIRS Brainstorm new ideas for programs or products to help the environment in your country.**

B **IN GROUPS Discuss which ideas are practical. Use the Confident Communicator box to help you.**

A: The government could create a law that requires all buildings to have living walls.
B: If they did that, it would be too expensive for a lot of people.
A: That's true. What if just big companies had to do it?
C: I think that's an awesome idea! It wouldn't be too hard, and it would help with air pollution.

CONFIDENT COMMUNICATOR
KEEP TALKING

To comment on good or unusual ideas, use the following phrases:
Good ideas: *What a* **cool / awesome / brilliant** *idea!*
Unusual ideas: *That's a* **(very) weird / bizarre / different / strange** *idea!*

Language and Life

Global Competence – Environmental Issues

A 5.05 **Read the blog. What is the blogger's main point?**

a Governments should do more to help the environment.
b Individual people and communities can only help the environment in very small ways.
c Individual people and communities can help the environment a lot.

Evan the Eco Guy—Micro-Ecology

How often have you heard or said this about a problem: "Why don't *they* do something?" Who is *they*? In the case of environmental problems, *they* probably refers to the government or to the world in general. But what if we stopped saying *they* and started saying *we*? There are many things that we, the people, can do to reduce global warming and to help the environment in general.

First, there are many small things that individual people and families can do. If we all tried to save energy, we would use less oil and gas, and there would be less carbon in the atmosphere. There are some very easy ways to save energy. Turn off lights when you are not in a room. Turn off your computer at night. Do several errands when you go out in your car, and offer to do errands for other people in your family. Share rides to school or work with family or friends. Try to buy locally produced food and other products. There are also many things that we can all do to produce less trash. Use reusable shopping bags for all types of shopping. When you buy fast food, don't take too many napkins, and don't take plastic forks if you are going to eat the food at home.

Neighborhoods and communities can also do many things to help the environment. Community gardens help in several ways. First, plants put oxygen into the air and use carbon dioxide. Second, if people eat food from local gardens, they are not eating food that was transported by trucks or planes. Third, flowers attract insects and birds that pollinate plants. Communities can also set up neighborhood websites to share rides, recycle things like clothes or toys, or organize volunteers to pick up trash in local parks and recycle it. If we did a little more as individuals and communities, we could have a very positive effect on our environment.

B IN PAIRS **Answer the questions about the blog in A.**

1. According to the blogger, who does the word *they* usually refer to?
2. What would happen if everyone did a few small things to save energy?
3. How do you think sharing rides and doing errands for other people can help save energy?
4. Why do you think buying local products helps the environment?
5. How many reasons does the writer give for having community gardens?
6. How can people use neighborhood websites?

C **Look at some ideas for individual environmental projects. Check (✓) the *Yes* column for the ones that you already do or think you would do. For the ones that you would not do, write the number of the reason in the *No* column.**

	Yes	No	Reason Not to Do It
Use a carpool to go to work or school.			1 I don't think it works.
Plant trees or flowers.			2 It's expensive.
Use my own coffee cup or water bottle.			3 It takes too much time or effort.
Combine errands with friends and neighbors.			4 I don't know how/where to do it.
Use my own shopping bags.			5 I won't remember to do it.
Use energy-efficient light bulbs.			6 I don't want to do it.
Take shorter showers.			7 It isn't possible in my area.
Have a vegetarian day once a week.			
Save gift wrapping and use it for other gifts.			
Buy locally produced food and products.			

D **IN GROUPS** **Discuss your answers to C. Encourage your classmates to take action and try some of the ideas.**

A: It's easy to buy local products. For example, you can shop at the farmer's market.
B: We should take shorter showers. Why? Because it saves water, and it also takes less time!
C: It doesn't matter if you don't know how. If you look online, you can find out how to …
D: It's really important to … because …

E **With your group, think of more ideas to take action and help the environment. Make a list of ideas.**

F **Share your ideas with the class and discuss whether you think they would work in your community. Agree on the top three ideas.**

A: I think a community garden is a great idea.
B: Me too. We could sell the vegetables we grow.
C: I'm not sure. You would need lots of volunteers.

G **Discuss the questions.**

1 Was it easy or difficult to encourage people to try your ideas? Why or why not?
2 How can we encourage people to change their every day habits?
3 What global impact would there be if we made these changes?

MAKE IT DIGITAL

Go online to find out what town or neighborhood programs already exist in your community and volunteer to help. If there are no initiatives, use social media to organize one.

VOCABULARY review

SCORE: / 10

A Complete the sentences with words from the box.

fines	melts	provide	rubber	traps
fog	nets	reduce	steel	weather

1 We need to ______________ our use of fossil fuels.
2 ______________ is a cloud close to the ground.
3 We're having bad ______________ this week—a lot of storms.
4 Cities ______________ many services, such as trash collection and electricity.
5 The greenhouse effect happens when carbon dioxide ______________ heat in the atmosphere.
6 Companies that pollute should have to pay ______________.
7 ______________ are often used to catch large numbers of fish.
8 If the ice in the Arctic and Antarctic ______________, sea levels will rise to dangerous levels.
9 ______________ is a natural material used to make things like tires and flip-flops.
10 ______________ is a type of very strong metal.

GRAMMAR review

SCORE: / 10

A Complete the blog entry with the correct forms of the verbs in parentheses.

Earth Citizen

I hope everyone **1** ______________ (read) this. If we **2** ______________ (not do) something about climate change in the near future, it **3** ______________ (be) too late. Years ago, scientists told us that if we didn't stop using so much fossil fuel, there **4** ______________ (be) terrible consequences. It isn't too late yet. If we used less fossil fuel, there **5** ______________ (be) less carbon in the atmosphere. Climate change would happen more slowly if we **6** ______________ (create) stronger laws, but unless we **7** ______________ (act) soon, we **8** ______________ (not have) our beautiful planet anymore! I wish everyone **9** ______________ (understand) the importance of this problem, and I wish world leaders **10** ______________ (work) together in the future to save our planet.

16–20 correct: You can talk about environmental issues and offer solutions. You can use conditionals for present and future hopes and wishes.
0–15 correct: Look again at the Vocabulary and Grammar sections in the unit.

TOTAL SCORE: / 20

WHAT DO YOU KNOW NOW? Look back at page 47 and add the words you know now to the boxes.

STUDY SKILLS IMPROVING READING SPEED

Take the quiz about improving reading speed. Go to **Study Skills** on page 131 to find the answers. Then learn more about improving reading speed.

1 It is always important to read things quickly.
a True **b** False

2 Reading aloud is always beneficial for reading.
a True **b** False

3 Which two of the following are active reading strategies?
a scanning **b** questioning **c** skimming **d** predicting

4 Moving your finger down the page as you read can help you read faster.
a True **b** False

UNIT 6 Moments in Time

WHAT DO YOU ALREADY KNOW?

1 Think about events, inventions, and people in history. Write the words.

2 IN PAIRS Share and compare your ideas. Add more words to your lists.

The past

VIDEO

DISCUSS & SHARE

3 IN GROUPS Watch the video and answer the question.

SYM Do you wait for inspiration or do you do your work step by step?

In this unit, you will ...

- compare different generational use of technology, share your opinions about inventions, write quiz questions about people in history.
- use thinking skills: predict, evaluate, and question.
- read about technological change.
- use strategies to keep a conversation going when you do not know a word, interrupt politely, and express interest and surprise.
- use decision-making skills to make judgments about UNESCO sites.
- follow an archaeologist to learn about this job and the skills needed for this industry.

READING

A 6.01 READING SKILL—Scan **Check (✓) the commercial technology events that you think happened before 1900. Then scan the first paragraph of the magazine article to check your answers.**

- ☐ the first electric taxis
- ☐ the first commercial flight
- ☐ the first commercial telephone company
- ☐ the first movie theater
- ☐ the first locomotive passenger train
- ☐ the first radio station

In Just 20 Years...

By the end of the 19th century, the Industrial Revolution had changed the world forever, and technology has continued to make many improvements since then. The first two decades of both the 20th and the 21st centuries brought life-changing progress in technology. From 1900 to 1920, there were enormous changes, especially in communications and transportation. Of course, there had already been innovations in these areas when the 20th century began. For example, the first passenger train powered by a locomotive had started in 1825 in England, but the huge expansion of the railroads in the US and Europe came in the 20th century. The first commercial telephone company opened in 1878, but at the beginning of the 20th century, the telephone had not yet become widely available to the public. Most surprisingly, there were electric taxis in London by 1897, but automobiles became available to ordinary people with the invention of the assembly line in the 20th century. The first two decades of the 20th century also brought the first movie theater in 1905, the first commercial flight in 1914, and the first radio station in 1920.

In the first two decades of the 21st century, progress in information technology was particularly important. This "Digital Revolution" included two of the most important developments in communications since the telephone — smartphones and the creation of social media platforms. The first social media network was Friendster in 2002, and the first modern smartphone was the iPhone in 2007. Entertainment technology also changed enormously from the close of the 20th century to the first decades of the 21st century. Some of the major 21st-century inventions so far have been wireless headsets in 2002, YouTube and internet radio in 2005, e-readers in 2007, and virtual reality headsets in 2016. It is hard to imagine where digital technology will take us by the end of the 21st century!

B IN PAIRS **Read the article. Then answer the questions.**

1. What two types of revolution does the article mention? When did they happen?
2. How many centuries are mentioned in the article?
3. What types of technology are mentioned in the first paragraph?
4. What were two important developments in communications in the 21st century?
5. How did entertainment technology change in the 21st century?
6. Did most of the progress in IT mentioned in the article happen in the first or the second decade of the 21st century?

GLOSSARY

innovation (n): a new idea, method, or object
assembly line (n): a system for making things in a factory in which each worker or machine adds one part
decade (n): 10 years

C IN GROUPS THINKING SKILL—Predict **The writer says it's hard to imagine where digital technology will take us by the end of the 21st century. Predict what technology you think will exist by the end of this century.**

A: I think people will have … *B: I don't think so, but I think … / Maybe there will be …*

VOCABULARY

A Scan the article in READING A and write a word with a similar meaning for each of these words.

1 close (n): ______________ [para. 1]
2 progress (n): ______________ [para. 1]
3 huge (adj): ______________ [para. 1]
4 especially (adv): ______________ [para. 2]
5 invention (n): ______________ [para. 2]
6 important (adj): ______________ [para. 2]

GRAMMAR past perfect

A Label the underlined times or events *1* or *2* to indicate which happened first.

1 By the end of the 19th century, the Industrial Revolution had changed the world forever …

2 Of course, there had already been innovations in these fields when the 20th century began.

3 …, but at the beginning of the 20th century, the telephone had not yet become widely available to the public.

B Choose the correct options.

1 Use the **simple past** / **past perfect** to talk about an action that happened before another action in the past.
2 Use the **simple past** / **past perfect** to talk about an action that happened after another action in the past.
3 Form the past perfect with *have* / *had* + a past participle.

For more practice, go to page 149.

C Complete the paragraph with the simple past or past perfect forms of the verbs in parentheses.

I was born in 1980, so I've seen a lot of changes in technology in my life. When I **1** ______________ (start) college in 1998, I **2** ______________ (use) a computer, but I **3** ______________ (not send) an email because I didn't have internet. I **4** ______________ (get) internet service at home in 2000, and by 2002, when I **5** ______________ (graduate) from college, I **6** ______________ (learn) to use email, and I **7** ______________ even ______________ (join) the Friendster social media network! I **8** ______________ (think) I was very modern! 🙄

D Think about technology the year you became a teenager. Write three things you had already done and three things you hadn't done yet at that time. Share your sentences with a group or a partner. Who used more technology as a preteen?

I had already learned to use the internet.
I hadn't bought a tablet yet.

SPEAKING

A IN PAIRS **Make a list of as many things as you can think of that people in the 21st century frequently do online, such as make plane reservations, buy things, or ask for advice about problems. Use the Confident Communicator box to help you.**

B Make a list of things you think your parents had and had not done online by 2000.

C IN GROUPS **Compare your lists. Whose parents had already done a lot of things online by 2000? Which things have they now done online that they hadn't done in 2000?**

CONFIDENT COMMUNICATOR
KEEP TALKING

To continue the conversation when you don't know a word, use the following phrases to communicate what you mean:
I can't think of the exact word, but It's similar to … / It's a kind of …
What's the word I'm thinking of? It means …

Inventions Big and Small

LISTENING

A IN PAIRS **Look at these 21st-century inventions. Match each picture (a–f) to a category (1–6), according to your opinions.**

a 
a car that drives itself

b 
a waterproof notepad for the shower

c 
a hammock for feet

d 
a light that creates a bike lane

e 
a camera that takes 360° photos

f 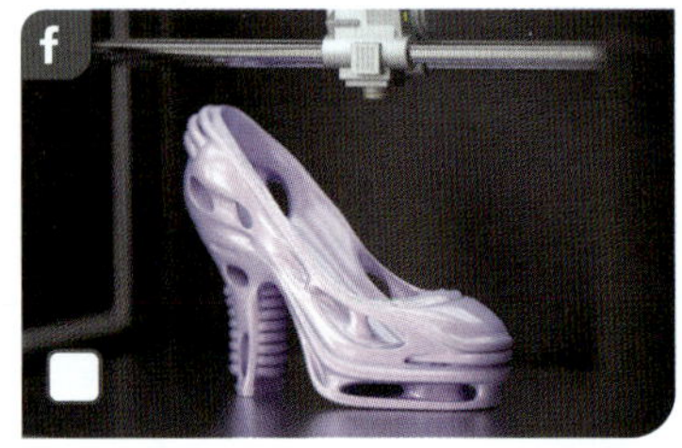
a printer that makes 3-D objects

1 the most unusual invention ______
2 the most amusing invention ______
3 the most exciting invention ______
4 the most worrying invention ______
5 the most useful invention ______
6 the most useless invention ______

B 6.02 **Listen to the street interviews. Check (✓) the things in A that the speakers mention. Make notes of words the speakers use to describe each invention.**

C 6.02 IN PAIRS LISTENING SKILL—Listen for supporting details **Listen again. Then answer the questions.**

1 Why is the first man worried about 3-D printers? ______________________
2 Why is the first woman excited about 360° cameras? ______________________
3 How does the second man feel about many 21st-century inventions? ______________________
4 What is the second woman worried about with driverless cars? ______________________

D IN GROUPS THINKING SKILL—Evaluate **Assess the opinions of the people who were interviewed in B. Do you agree or disagree with their opinions? Discuss.**

VOCABULARY *–ed* and *–ing* adjectives

A Read the examples from LISTENING B. Then choose the correct options to complete the rules.

A: I'm pretty worried about some of the recent inventions.
B: To me, the invention that is the most worrying so far is the 3-D printer.
A: I'm really amused by some of the things that have been invented.
B: Yes, I guess some inventions are more amusing than useful.

1 Adjectives like *worried* and *worrying* are formed from **nouns / verbs**.
2 Adjectives with *–ing* are used to describe **something or someone / a feeling about something or someone**.
3 Adjectives with *–ed* are used to describe **something or someone / a feeling about something or someone**.

B **Choose the correct adjective forms.**

I'm not sure about driverless cars. Personally, I think driving is **1 amazed / amazing**, so I would be **2 disappointed / disappointing** if I couldn't do it anymore. I understand that there are many people who would like to have a driverless car. How **3 relaxed / relaxing** to sit in your car and read or sleep! I definitely get **4 bored / boring** driving in traffic, and it would be very **5 entertained / entertaining** to watch a video or play a game on your phone while your car drives, but we need to be patient and wait until the technology is more advanced.

MAKE IT YOURS

Some people think technology is amazing. Others are terrified. How do the different types of technology around you make you feel?

GRAMMAR defining relative clauses

A **Underline the word or phrase that each relative pronoun in bold refers to.**

1 I'm on a street **where** lots of young people hang out on Saturday evenings. ____________

2 If there's a time **when** people can make most of their own products, ... ____________

3 There are some inventors **who** are creating some pretty amusing things! ____________

4 ... to me, the invention **that** is the most worrying so far is the 3-D printer. ____________

5 The 21st-century device **which** does everything is the phone. ____________

B **Now label the sentences in A *person*, *place*, *time*, or *object* according to what the relative pronoun refers to. Then choose the correct option in the rule.**

You can use *that* / *when* instead of *who* or *which*.

For more practice, go to page 150.

C **Complete the sentences with relative pronouns. Then think of a response to each sentence.**

1 Give an example of a time ____________ you bought something that you were disappointed with.

2 Name the main places ____________ you shop, apart from online.

3 Give examples of some recent innovations ____________ you have used lately.

4 Think of a person ____________ has been very important in the first decades of the 21st century.

D IN PAIRS **Share your responses in C with your partner.**

SPEAKING

A **Answer the questionnaire.**

Opinion Poll on 21st-Century Innovations and Inventions

1 What recent invention or innovation is the most exciting to you?

2 Are there any modern inventions that you find confusing and hard to use?

3 Was there a time when you were disappointed by a new product?

4 Is there an inventor or innovator who is a role model to you?

5 What possible future inventions are you interested in or excited about?

B IN GROUPS **Share your opinions about the poll in A.**

CONFIDENT COMMUNICATOR

KEEP TALKING

To interrupt someone politely, use these phrases:

Excuse me, can/may I interrupt?

Just a second. Can I ask you a question?

Sorry, can you repeat that?

LISTENING

A Match the people in the pictures (a–d) with the things they did (1–4).

a Michel Krieger

b Mario Molina

c Dr. Christiaan Barnard

d Mary Anderson

1 identified the danger of chlorofluorocarbons in the atmosphere. ______
2 performed the first heart transplant. ______
3 co-founded Instagram. ______
4 invented windshield wipers. ______

GLOSSARY

transplant (n): a medical operation to take an organ from one person's body and put it into another person's body
cardiac surgeon (n): a doctor who operates on human hearts
defect (n): a fault or problem in something
pneumonia (n): a serious illness of the lungs and respiratory system

B 6.03 THINKING SKILL—Question **Predict the types of information in the podcast about a famous person. Write questions to ask about that information. Then listen and write the answers to your questions.**

Questions	Answers
1 What was his name?	______
2 ______	______
3 ______	______
4 ______	______

C 6.03 LISTENING SKILL—Listen for numerical information **Listen again and write information about each number in your notebook.**

1 1922 **2** 1967 **3** 54 **4** 18 **5** 7,000

D IN PAIRS **Compare your notes in C. Explain in your own words the importance of each number.**

VOCABULARY adjective suffixes

A Add the suffixes *–ful*, *–less*, *–able*, and *–ible* to form adjectives from LISTENING B. Then check your work with a partner. Some words can go in more than one column.

	–ful	–less	–able	–ible
1 success–	*successful*			
2 cap–				
3 hope–				
4 incred–				
5 thank–				

B Match the adjectives in A with the definitions below.

1 ______________________: grateful or happy about something
2 ______________________: unlikely that a situation will succeed or improve
3 ______________________: achieving the result you want
4 ______________________: believing that something good will happen
5 ______________________: very, very good
6 ______________________: able to do something

PRONUNCIATION stress in multisyllable adjectives

A 6.04 Listen and underline the stressed syllable in each word.

hopeful capable thankful successful preventable incredible

WRITING

A Read the short biographical essay. What was unusual about Valentina Tereshkova?

Valentina Tereshkova

a In 1960, the idea of humans in space was still a dream. By the end of 1961, the dream had become reality with Soviet cosmonaut Yuri Gagarin. In that decade, science and space travel were dominated by men. **b** However, on June 16, 1963, cosmonaut Valentina Tereshkova became the first woman to travel into space.

c Valentina Tereshkova was born in 1937 in a small town about 277 km. from Moscow. In 1954, she started working at a textile factory, and around that time, she learned to parachute. Because of her parachuting experience, in 1962 she was chosen to train as a cosmonaut. On her space flight in 1963, Tereshkova orbited the Earth 48 times in a little less than three days. When she returned to Earth, Tereshkova parachuted over 6,000 meters from her spacecraft to Earth! **d** As the first woman in space, Valentina Tereshkova was a pioneer for women in space travel and for professional women in general.

B Read the tips for writing a biography. Match the underlined parts (a–d) of the text in A to the tips (1–4).

1 Choose a specific angle, e.g., the first to do something, and present it in your introduction. ______
2 Write an interesting first sentence to introduce the topic. ______
3 Restate your angle in the conclusion of your essay. ______
4 Give basic biographical facts about the person's life. Include some interesting details. ______

C Make notes to prepare to write a short biographical essay. Use the tips in B as a guide.

D Write your biography. Then share it with a partner. Help each other with ideas for improvements.

SPEAKING

A IN PAIRS Match the historical facts (a–d) with the people (1–4).

1 Roger Bannister (UK) ______
2 Junko Tabei (Japan) ______
3 Gabriela Mistral (Chile) ______
4 Leonardo da Vinci (Italy) ______

a the first woman who climbed Mt. Everest
b the first person who ran a mile in less than four minutes
c the first to understand the circulation of blood in the body
d the first Latin American author to win the Nobel Prize for Literature

B IN PAIRS Write a quiz similar to the one in A. Your quiz should have four to six items.

CONFIDENT COMMUNICATOR
KEEP TALKING

Use these phrases to express interest:
Really? *Oh, I didn't know that.* *That's interesting.* *Huh.*
Use these phrases to express surprise:
Seriously?! *That's so cool!*

Language and Life

Decison Making – UNESCO Sites

A 6.05 **Read the information about UNESCO sites. Then choose *True* or *False*.**

UNESCO: Preserving Our Heritage

The main role of the United Nations Educational, Scientific, and Cultural Organization (UNESCO) is to encourage international collaboration, and to promote global security and peace. One way that UNESCO achieves this is through the preservation of sites of great cultural or national importance. This develops respect for those sites among the citizens of those countries. It also educates tourists about those sites and encourages them to discover the beauty of that country's culture.

Tourists can find out more about all of the UNESCO's sites by going to the World Heritage List, which can be found on the official UNESCO website. Currently, there are almost 1,100 sites on this list, including national parks, forests, islands, temples, and houses. Some of the sites are very well-known, like the Great Wall in China and Machu Picchu in Peru, but there are many sites that are well-known only within the countries where they are located. It is possible to use the World Heritage List as a way to find out more about your own country, or to inspire future vacations.

To be included on the World Heritage List, a site needs to be considered of universal importance. UNESCO has created a set of criteria to select World Heritage sites. These criteria examine the site's cultural importance, as well as its natural beauty. There are a total of ten criteria that UNESCO considers in the site selection process, and a site has to have at least one of them to be selected. Some of the criteria are:

1. Be an example of an important cultural tradition of the past or present
2. Be an example of amazing human creativity
3. Be an example of a culture's use of land or sea that is positive for the environment
4. Have incredible natural beauty
5. Represent an important period in the Earth's history
6. Represent great achievements in technology, architecture, the arts, town planning, or landscape design

Khajuraho Temple, Madhya Pradesh, a UNESCO World Heritage site

1	One purpose of UNESCO is to educate people about different cultures.	True / False
2	All UNESCO sites are buildings.	True / False
3	All UNESCO sites are very famous.	True / False
4	A site has to have most of the criteria to be chosen by UNESCO.	True / False
5	Human creativity is important to UNESCO.	True / False
6	Ecology and the environment are factors in UNESCO selections.	True / False

B **IN PAIRS** **Read about a recent UNESCO selection. Decide which of the criteria in A you think UNESCO applied to this site.**

Chiribiquete National Park, Colombia—The Maloca of the Jaguar

The Chiribiquete National Park is the largest protected area in Colombia. The flat, table-top mountains are an unusual geological feature, and they give the park its dramatic beauty. There are rock shelters at the base of the mountains that have over 75,000 paintings dating from 20,000 BCE to the present. The paintings represent the powerful jaguar, and this is a sacred region for indigenous communities.

C **IN PAIRS** **You are going to choose a site in your country to propose as a UNESCO World Heritage Site. Follow the steps to help you make a good decision.**

Making Decisions with Criteria and Weight

1. Rate the six UNESCO criteria in column 1 from 1 to 3 points—3 being very important to you and 1 being the least important to you.
2. Think of a site or region in your country that might qualify for UNESCO. Add it to the table in column 2.
3. Rate your site from 1 to 3 for each of the six criteria (3—completely matches the criterion; 1—does not match the criterion very well).
4. Multiply each criterion by the rating. Add up the total points for each option.

1 UNESCO Criteria (1–3 points)	2 Site/Region: ______ (rating 1–3)	3 Weighting (criterion x rating)
1: ______ pt(s).		
2: ______ pt(s).		
3: ______ pt(s).		
4: ______ pt(s).		
5: ______ pt(s).		
6: ______ pt(s).		
	Total weighting score: ______	

D **IN GROUPS** **Present your UNESCO proposal to your group. Compare and evaluate weighting scores and decide which proposal is best for a UNESCO site. Present your proposal to the class.**

E **Discuss the questions.**

1. Do you think this is a useful way to help make decisions? Why or why not?
2. In what other situations might you use this ranking and rating system?

MAKE IT DIGITAL

Find out if there are any UNESCO World Heritage Sites in your country and if there are any sites proposed for the future.

VOCABULARY review

SCORE: / 10

A Choose the correct words.

I'm **1 thankless / thankful** that there are so many **2 capable / hopeful** people who invent useful things! Some are famous and **3 successful / entertaining** people like Bill Gates, but many are not famous at all. There are people who work at companies all over the world to give us **4 amazing / amazed** things like 3-D cameras and driverless cars. It's very **5 entertained / entertaining** to play video games or watch online videos, and someone had to invent that technology. However, being an inventor can be **6 boring / bored** because an inventor has to focus on very small details, and it takes a long time to invent something. Inventors are **7 disappointed / disappointing** when their inventions don't work very well, but sometimes an invention becomes a **8 capable / huge** success. A **9 huge / particularly** important invention in recent years was HD (high-definition) TV. This was an enormous **10 improvement / creation** in TV technology.

GRAMMAR review

SCORE: / 10

A Complete the sentences with the simple past or past perfect forms of the verbs in parentheses.

1. My dad ____________ (not have) a smartphone before I ____________ (give) him one for his birthday.
2. After I ____________ (save) enough money, I ____________ (buy) a small car.
3. When my dad ____________ (buy) his first car, he ____________ never ____________ (drive) a car!
4. At the beginning of the 21st century, many people ____________ (not use) the internet.
5. No one ____________ (hear) the term *social media* when the first social media network ____________ (begin) in 2002.

B Complete the sentences with *who, that, where, when,* and *which.*

1. Driverless cars are an innovation ____________ may change the transportation industry.
2. Tech companies are places ____________ there are a lot of creative people!
3. An AI specialist is a person ____________ works in artificial intelligence technology.
4. My dad was born in a decade ____________ a lot of important technology was invented.
5. There are millions of people in the world ____________ use the internet every day.

16–20 correct: You can talk about events in history and changes in the modern world.
You can use defining relative clauses and adjective suffixes.
0–15 correct: Look again at the Vocabulary and Grammar sections in the unit.

TOTAL SCORE: / 20

WHAT DO YOU KNOW NOW? Look back at page 57 and add the words you know now to the box.

FOLLOW A PRO ANCIENT CIVILIZATIONS

Take the quiz about ancient civilizations. Go to Follow A Pro on page 132 to find the answers. Then learn more about archeologists.

1 Cleopatra was …
a Greek. b Egyptian. c Roman.

2 According to a Roman legend, Rome's founder, Romulus, was raised by a …
a Greek woman. b goddess. c wolf.

3 The oldest civilization in the Americas was the …
a Olmec in Mexico. b Caral Supe in Peru. c Cherokee in the US.

4 One of the first medical centers was in …
a Persia (Iran), in the 6th century. b Athens, Greece, in the 12th century. c London, England, in the 16th century.

UNIT 1 STUDY SKILLS

A Read what students have to say about time management challenges. Which of the challenges do you face most often?

EFFECTIVE TIME MANAGEMENT

1 ______ Radu I guess social media is my biggest obstacle to getting things done. It's just too easy to take time out and see what my buddies are doing. Before I know where I am, I've gotten myself involved in some kind of debate, or—and this happens more often—find myself scrolling through the vacation pictures of someone I barely know.

2 ______ Deepali I find that I lose concentration too easily. I start off well, but after an hour I don't feel like I'm taking anything in anymore. How can I stay focused?

3 ______ Katia Time just disappears. It's always the same—I start off feeling like I have all the time in the world. Then it gets to deadline time and I have no idea where the days and hours have gone! I wind up doing everything too fast and my grades aren't great as a result.

4 ______ Roberto I feel like I spend a lot of time reading online. The internet's a huge place and it's easy to get lost. The problem is that I'm never sure if the stuff I'm reading is actually any good.

5 ______ Simone I can focus on my studies if there are no distractions. The problem is that I get so many messages from friends, and they might think it's rude if I don't reply right away. Well, it is a bit rude, isn't it?

B Match the problems in A (1–5) to the pieces of advice (a–e).

a Turn your phone off when you are studying, or keep it on silent.
b Reward yourself with social media time at the end of a study session, but go offline when you are trying to complete a task.
c Before you start reading an article online, make sure that it comes from a source that you can trust.
d Be systematic in planning your schedule. Decide what needs to be done urgently and what is not so important. Be realistic about how long it takes you to complete tasks, and leave yourself enough time.
e Study in short periods (45 minutes is realistic), and reward yourself with 5 to 10 minutes of relaxation between study periods.

MAKE IT HAPPEN

Make a study plan for the coming month with your assignment deadlines and the exam dates. Write down the days and times you will be in class and decide how much time you need for independent study. Include time for hobbies, relaxation, and sleep in your schedule. Compare your schedule with that of your partner and give your partner feedback.

C Complete the tips with words from the box. Can you think of two more strategies for managing your time effectively? Write them below.

deadlines	realistic	schedule

Make a list of all your **1** ______________. Write them on a calendar or in a planner so you can see how much time you have.
Be **2** ______________ about how long it takes you to do things. It's better to overestimate than underestimate.
Reward yourself for hard work by setting aside time for relaxation in your **3** ______________.
4 ____
5 ____

D IN PAIRS Talk about what you can do to become better at managing your time. Mention any specific challenges you face. Listen to your partner and offer advice based on what you have learned in this lesson.

E THINKING SKILL—Apply Explain why time management skills are so important in study, work, and life in general. Why does the "good time management skills" requirement appear so often in job advertisements?

Answers to the quiz on page 16
1 b and c 2 b 3 c 4 b

UNIT 2 FOLLOW A PRO

A Read about a wildlife photographer's job. Answer the questions below in your notebook.

A WILDLIFE PHOTOGRAPHER

Jeff Richards works as a freelance wildlife photographer.

"These days, everyone has a camera on their phone, and there are images all around us. If you're going to make a living as a wildlife photographer, you need to be able to take pictures that are different and that really stand out. And that means getting into an animal's habitat to get close to it. A wildlife photographer needs to be an expert at using photographic equipment, but you also need to understand animal behavior. When you understand an animal, you can look ahead, know where it's going to be and how it's going to act, and be ready to take your shot. Physical fitness is very important, too, since you may need to put yourself in an unusual position to get the shot that is going to sell.

When I'm not on a shoot, the rest of my time is spent editing images, contacting clients, and planning future trips. It takes a long time to build up a career in this very competitive area, so you need to understand how to run a business as well as having a good eye for a picture. You need to be patient when you're trying to get the right shot of an animal, and you need to apply the same patience to your career. It's not necessarily the right career for someone who wants instant success."

1 Why do your pictures need to stand out and be different?
2 What does a wildlife photographer need to be able to predict?
3 Why does it help to be physically fit?
4 Apart from photographic skills and knowledge of animals, what other area does a wildlife photographer need to understand?
5 Why might this not be a good career for someone who wants instant success?

B Discuss the questions as a class.

1 What do you imagine is the hardest thing about being a wildlife photographer?
2 Do you think you have the right skills to be a wildlife photographer? What could you do or not do?

VIDEO

WATCH THE VIDEO AND FOLLOW A MARINE BIOLOGIST.

C IN GROUPS Answer the questions.

1 What does the person do? ____________________
2 Where does the person work? ____________________
3 What skills does the person need for the job? ____________________
4 What is the focus of the person's research? ____________________
5 On how many projects is the person currently working? ____________________
6 What is the most exciting part of the person's job? ____________________

D IN GROUPS Check your answers to the quiz on page 26 and discuss the questions.

1 Do you know anyone who works with animals? Explain what you think his or her job is like.
2 What other jobs working with animals do you know about?
3 What do you think are the most enjoyable things about working with animals? What are the least enjoyable?
4 What skills does a veterinarian need? Is it a career you would consider?
5 Are there any opportunities to work with animals where you live? If so, what are they?

Answers to the quiz on page 26
1 b 2 c 3 c 4 a

UNIT 3

STUDY SKILLS

A Read the conversation between Soren and Tania.

MAKING A PRESENTATION OR GIVING A TALK

Soren: How's your talk going, Tania? Are you nearly ready?
Tania: It's going well, I think! I'm doing mine on the advantages and disadvantages of artificial intelligence.
Soren: Wow. That's really interesting. So, are there more advantages or disadvantages?
Tania: Whoa, hold on! I haven't gotten to that part yet. Right now, I'm just writing the history.
Soren: That's just the history? That's over 30 pages! How will you remember all that?
Tania: Ha, ha! I won't! I'll just type the information on my presentation and read it to the audience. It's much easier than remembering it all.
Soren: I see. But didn't Mr. Elmwood say the talk should be 10 minutes maximum?
Tania: Yeah, I know! Don't worry, though, I talk really fast when I get excited about something!
Soren: Well, be careful you don't write too much, or you won't have time to say it all. I mean, look—you've written 30 pages and you haven't even started writing about the advantages and disadvantages yet.
Tania: That won't take long. I mean, everyone knows that there are only advantages to artificial intelligence, right? No one thinks there are disadvantages.
Soren: Well, you certainly seem confident.
Tania: I don't really get nervous about talks, especially when I'm talking about my favorite subject. It'll be great!

B Select four pieces of advice that you think would be most useful for Tania.

1 If possible, speak from notes written on note cards or from memory.
2 Choose a subject that you are interested in or feel strongly about.
3 Make sure your research and preparation are balanced.
4 Don't speak too fast. Pause and take a breath after each point you make.
5 Be aware and respectful of the fact that some audience members may not share your point of view.

C Match the tips about oral presentations in B (1–5) to the explanations (a–e).

a This means that your talk will flow better and that you will be able to make eye contact with your audience. ______
b Audience members are likely to stop listening if they feel their point of view is not being respected. ______
c This will make you seem calmer and more professional. Your voice will sound stronger, too. ______
d This will show that you are well prepared and not biased. ______
e This means that your enthusiasm will be noticeable and that people will enjoy listening to you. ______

D IN PAIRS Discuss your experiences giving talks. Talk about your strengths and weaknesses and decide what further tips you would add to the list in B. Think about the following points.

- Developing your main argument
- Providing a clear structure
- Opening and summing up
- Including effective visual aids
- Answering questions
- Engaging with the audience

E THINKING SKILLS—Apply Think about a memorable talk you have listened to. Why was it memorable? What techniques did the speaker use to engage with the audience?

MAKE IT HAPPEN

Prepare an oral presentation on something you are interested in. Use the tips from this lesson to help you plan, structure, and deliver your talk.

Answers to the quiz on page 36
1 c 2 b 3 a 4 a

UNIT 4

FOLLOW A PRO

A Read about a PR professional's job. Answer the questions below in your notebook.

A PR PROFESSIONAL

Companies have messages about their brands that they want to communicate to members of the public. They use advertising for some of those messages. They also employ or hire PR (public relations) professionals. PR professionals work with journalists and other people in the media. They are responsible for communicating positive stories about a company and its products.

PR professionals need to be good at networking. They need contacts in many areas of the media. They need to know who they can persuade to run a story in a way that makes their business look good. This is particularly important when something negative happens to the company, such as people losing their jobs. The PR professional is the person who tries to explain the reason behind what is happening in a positive way.

Successful PR professionals have to express themselves clearly and have very good writing skills. They spend a lot of time producing press releases, fact sheets, and other documents that give journalists the starting point for their reports and articles. They can make a big difference to the stories that appear in the media. PR professionals also tell the stories behind their companies and brands through events such as press conferences or open houses. The PR professional is an important connection between a business and the public.

1 What is the main role of a PR professional?
2 Why does a PR professional need to be good at networking?
3 When is a PR professional's job particularly important?
4 What communication skills does a PR professional need to have?
5 How do PR professionals help journalists?

B Discuss the questions as a class.

1 What do you think PR professionals enjoy most about their job?
2 Would you be a good PR professional? Why or why not?

VIDEO

WATCH THE VIDEO AND FOLLOW A TRANSLATOR/INTERPRETER.

C IN GROUPS Answer the questions.

1 What is the person's job? ____________________
2 What skills does the person need for the job? ____________________
3 Where has the person worked as a translator? ____________________
4 How many languages does the person speak? ____________________
5 What is the person's first language? ____________________
6 Why does the person prefer doing interpretation instead of translation? ____________________

D IN GROUPS Check your answers to the quiz on page 46 and discuss the questions.

1 What careers in communication do you know about?
2 Would you be interested in any of those careers? If so, which ones?
3 Do you know anyone who works in communication? If so, what do you think his or her job is like?
4 What personal qualities do you need to work in PR?
5 What qualifications do you need to work in PR?

Answers to the quiz on page 46
1 c 2 b 3 a 4 a

UNIT 5 STUDY SKILLS

A Time yourself as you read this text as quickly as you can. What environmental problem is described in the text? What possible solutions are given?

IMPROVING READING SPEED

Let's imagine a typical morning. You leave your home for college or work. On the way, you stop and buy yourself a bottle of water. Perhaps you'll be given a plastic straw to drink it with. At lunch, you choose a nice healthy salad in a plastic box—or a sandwich wrapped in plastic. Maybe you'll eat the salad with plastic cutlery. On the way home, you'll stop off at the store for some groceries, probably also wrapped in plastic. All this plastic is used just once before you throw it away and forget all about it.

Here's the problem: plastic never fully biodegrades. It simply breaks down into smaller particles, which can be absorbed by our bodies. This has serious effects on our health; scientific research has linked plastic to cancer, birth defects, infertility, and a weakened immune system. Plastic is also a huge problem for marine animals, who can get tangled up in plastic rope or choke on pieces of plastic packaging. One million sea birds and 100,000 marine mammals are killed every year by plastic in our oceans.

In fact, 50% of plastic is used just once and then thrown away. Single-use plastic is probably one of the easiest things we could cut out of our lives to make a really big difference. Carry your own thermal flask for your coffee or hot drink, and carry your own water bottle. When shopping, try to choose as many items as you can that are not wrapped in plastic. There are lots of online challenges you can take part in to help you get motivated—or why not try a "no single-use plastic" challenge with a friend? You could also ask your college campus and local businesses to become "no single-use plastic" zones.

If each one of us committed to cutting out single-use plastic, we could fix one of the most serious environmental problems of our time.

B Match the sentence halves to make tips about improving reading speed.

1. Reading improves with practice, so you should _____
2. If you move your finger down the page while you read, _____
3. Active reading strategies such as predicting will _____
4. Putting a colored filter over the page can _____
5. Reading larger chunks of text at one time _____
6. If a nonfiction text looks hard, you should _____

a. you will train your eyes to move more quickly down the text.
b. start with something easier on the same subject.
c. make the words easier to read.
d. help you find the information you are looking for more quickly.
e. is less tiring for your eyes and will help you to read for longer periods.
f. look for subjects that interest you and read more for pleasure.

C Read the text in A again. This time, try to use as many of the tips from B as you can.

D IN PAIRS Which of the tips do you find most useful? Discuss your ideas with a partner.

Malin: I followed the tip about moving my finger down the page as I read. That definitely helped.

Theo: I tried reading larger chunks of text at one time, but I don't think it made a difference. I forgot what I had read!

Malin: I'm going to try that idea next time!

MAKE IT HAPPEN

Work with a partner. Look online and choose a text at an appropriate level that you think your partner would find interesting. Ask your partner to read the text using some of the tips outlined in these lessons. Share your findings in a group.

E THINKING SKILLS—Apply What makes a person a good reader? Apart from reading speed, what other ways can we use to measure our skills in this area?

Answers to the quiz on page 56
1 b 2 b 3 b and d 4 a

UNIT 6

FOLLOW A PRO

A **Read about an archeologist. Answer the questions below in your notebook.**

AN ARCHEOLOGIST

Many people think archeologists work outside, discovering the secrets of ancient civilizations in the mountains of Peru or the deserts of Egypt. Well, that's true, but is archeology really just about that? Archeology is a part of the larger field of anthropology, which is the study of human culture. Archeologists study structures and objects from ancient civilizations to try to understand what the ancient cultures were like and how ancient people lived. To be an archeologist, you will need a master's degree or a PhD. Your studies will include a large amount of research and probably some fieldwork. The chance of making a great discovery is what most archeologists dream of. However, even when it happens, archeologists have to carefully analyze their findings, to prove their importance. If you want to find out more about archeology before you spend a lot of time and money getting advanced degrees, research what an archeologist does online. You need to understand that archeologists do not all work in exciting places. Most of us work at places like historic sites, national parks, museums, or universities. We also often do not have regular working hours. We might work seven days a week for several weeks if there is an important project. We also have to work in all kinds of weather at all times of day. Archeology is an interesting job, and sometimes it's exciting, but you have to study a lot to become an archeologist, and you have to work very hard when you get a job!

1 What field is archeology a part of?
2 What do archeologists study? Why?
3 What do archeologists most want to achieve?
4 What is a good way to find out more about archeology before you decide to study it?
5 Where do archeologists work?

B **Discuss the questions as a class.**

1 In what ways is archeology a hard job?
2 Is archeology an important field in your country?

VIDEO

WATCH THE VIDEO AND FOLLOW A MECHANICAL ENGINEER.

C **IN GROUPS Answer the questions.**

1 What does the person do? ______
2 What skills does the person need for the job? ______
3 Where does the person often work? ______
4 What kind of special equipment does the person use? ______
5 Does the person work alone or in a team? ______
6 Is the person happy with the job? Why? ______

D **IN GROUPS Check your answers to the quiz on page 66 and discuss the questions.**

1 What old or ancient civilizations were in your country? Have you ever visited any of their sites? If so, which ones?
2 What other archeological or historical sites in the world would you like to visit?

Answers to the quiz on page 66
1 a 2 c 3 b 4 a

Irregular Verbs

Infinitive	Simple past	Past participle
be	was/were	been
become	became	become
begin	began	begun
break	broke	broken
bring	brought	brought
build	built	built
buy	bought	bought
catch	caught	caught
choose	chose	chosen
come	came	come
cost	cost	cost
cut	cut	cut
do	did	done
draw	drew	drawn
drink	drank	drunk
drive	drove	driven
eat	ate	eaten
fall	fell	fallen
feed	fed	fed
feel	felt	felt
find	found	found
fly	flew	flown
get	got	gotten
give	gave	given
go	went	gone
grow	grew	grown
hang	hung	hung
have	had	had
hear	heard	heard
hit	hit	hit
hold	held	held
hurt	hurt	hurt
keep	kept	kept
know	knew	known
leave	left	left
let	let	let
lose	lost	lost
make	made	made
meet	met	met
pay	paid	paid
put	put	put
read	read	read
ride	rode	ridden
ring	rang	rung
rise	rose	risen
run	ran	run
say	said	said
see	saw	seen
sell	sold	sold
send	sent	sent
set	set	set
sing	sang	sung
sit	sat	sat
speak	spoke	spoken
stand	stood	stood
stick	stuck	stuck
take	took	taken
teach	taught	taught
tell	told	told
think	thought	thought
throw	threw	thrown
understand	understood	understood
wake	woke	woken
wear	wore	worn
win	won	won
write	wrote	written

Pronunciation Symbols

Vowels

ɪ	did
ɛ	bed
æ	bad
ʌ	cup
ʊ	book
ə	banana
i	feed
ɑ	father, box
ɔ	tall
u	student, food
ɝ	shirt, birthday
eɪ	date, table
aɪ	cry, eye
ɔɪ	boy
oʊ	comb, post
aʊ	about, how

Consonants

p	park, happy
b	back, hobby
t	tea
d	die
k	came, kitchen, quarter
g	game, go
f	face, photographer
V	vegetable
θ	thing, math
ð	then, that
s	city, summer
z	please, goes
ʃ	she, shop
ʒ	leisure
h	hot, who
tʃ	chicken, watch
dʒ	jacket, orange
m	men
n	sun, know
ŋ	sung, singer
w	week, white
r	rain, writer
l	light, long
j	yes, use, music

Grammar Review

A **Complete the news report with the simple past or the past progressive form of the verbs in parentheses.**

There was a fire last night at 10:20 p.m. on East Coast Road. While Jon and Lisa Hawes **1** ______________ (watch) TV in their living room, their five-year-old son **2** ______________ (play) with matches in his bedroom. He **3** ______________ (light) a small fire and then, afraid, **4** ______________ (run) into the bathroom. While his parents **5** ______________ (come) to check on him, they **6** ______________ (smell) smoke. They **7** ______________ (try) to put the fire out, but it was already too big. They found their son, **8** ______________ (call) the fire department, and got out of the house safely.

B **Choose the correct options.**

Tyler: I really like your apartment. It gets **1 any / a lot of** light.

Miguel: Yeah, but there isn't **2 enough / too many** space for all my stuff. And I'd like to move **3 somebody / somewhere** closer to school.

Tyler: But this is a great neighborhood. There are **4 some / any** great restaurants and cafés here.

Miguel: I know, but there's **5 too many / too much** noise around here on the weekends. It feels like **6 anybody / everyone** is out on the street at night.

Tyler: You live alone, right? Have you ever thought about getting a roommate?

Miguel: I've considered it **7 a few / a little** times, but I really like living by **8 myself / ourselves**.

C **Complete the sentences with the correct superlative form of the adjective in parentheses.**

1. My cat is the ______________ (lazy) animal I've ever seen.
2. That was the ______________ (risk) thing I've ever done.
3. Rush hour is the ______________ (bad) time to get a seat on the bus.
4. Craig is the ______________ (creative) person in class.
5. Maria is the ______________ (kind) of my three sisters.
6. Ines is the ______________ (good) person to have as a study partner.

D **Rewrite the sentences to include the verb in parentheses.**

1. You are not allowed to come in. (can't)
   ____
2. Do you want to go with me? (would)
   ____
3. I'll possibly be late to the ceremony. (may)
   ____
4. Will you book a hotel room for me? (could)
   ____
5. I don't think I'll be able to come. (might)
   ____
6. Our flight lands in 30 minutes. (will)
   ____

E Complete the sentences with the simple past or the present perfect form of the verb in parentheses.

Although he is just a teenager, Brandon Iverson **1** ________ (be) a businessman for much of his life. At age 10, he and a friend **2** ________ (sell) old toys and games online. When he was 13, they **3** ________ (establish) their own financial education company. A year later, they **4** ________ (publish) a book on how to succeed as a young entrepreneur. They **5** ________ (make) a lot of money since then. A few years ago, Brandon **6** ________ (start) another online company selling T-shirts, jogging pants, and hoodies. The company **7** ________ (do) well since its launch. Recently, he **8** ________ (become) a popular speaker at schools around the country, and he is enjoying this new venture.

F Unscramble and write the sentences.

1 Jesse / degree / gotten / yet / hasn't / his / .
____

2 ever / Lila / promotion / a / gotten / has / ?
____

3 here / since / worked / 2017 / has / Peter / .
____

4 applied / Erica / for / already / job / has / the / .
____

5 our / read / I / just / benefits / about / have / .
____

6 been / Tina / has / month / team / a / leader / for / .
____

G Choose the correct option.

1 Many people are interested in **cooking** / **to cook** these days.
2 Why doesn't Claire want **flying** / **to fly** a kite with her friends?
3 Henri enjoys **making** / **to make** things with wood.
4 David really dislikes **cleaning** / **to clean** his apartment.
5 We really hope **seeing** / **to see** you at the park this weekend.
6 **Having** / **To have** a potluck meal sounds like a great idea!
7 Where did you and Ethan decide **going** / **to go** last night?
8 Would you like **coming** / **to come** over for a barbecue tonight?

H Complete the sentences with the correct form of the verb in parentheses.

1 Fur coats ________ (not wear) much nowadays.
2 Children may develop health problems if they ________ (eat) too much food.
3 These days, most hotel reservations ________ (make) online.
4 If we ________ (not be) friends, I would be angry with you.
5 When my parents were young, milk ________ (sell) in bottles.
6 If the weather doesn't improve, we ________ (not have) a picnic.
7 Cotton ________ (use) in clothing such as blue jeans and T-shirts.
8 I ________ (meet) my cousin at the airport tomorrow.

UNIT 1 — stative and dynamic verbs

Function

We use stative verbs such as *seem*, *know*, and *understand* to describe states. They are not usually used in progressive tenses. We use dynamic (action) verbs like *walk*, *run*, and *play* to describe actions. Some stative verbs, like *be*, *think*, and *have*, and verbs of the senses, like *see*, *smell*, *taste*, and *hear*, can also be used as dynamic verbs, though the meaning of the verb changes.

Form

Stative verbs	Dynamic verbs	Stative or dynamic
Juan **likes** climbing.	He **runs** every day.	I **think** she's amazing.
I **don't understand**.	**Don't laugh** at me.	She**'s thinking** about her work.
She **wants** to leave now.	We**'re playing** a video game.	This pasta **tastes** delicious.
I **don't know** how to play this.	They **are using** new technology.	She**'s tasting** the soup.

A Write *S* (stative) or *D* (dynamic) for each verb.

1 eat _____ **4** seem _____ **7** sleep _____ **10** believe _____
2 climb _____ **5** drink _____ **8** hate _____ **11** laugh _____
3 know _____ **6** want _____ **9** use _____ **12** understand _____

B Complete the sentences with the simple present or the present progressive form of the verb in parentheses.

1 I ____________________ (know) how to use this software.
2 ____________________ you ____________________ (like) to climb mountains?
3 My sister Sara ____________________ (have) a disability.
4 Our teacher ____________________ (think) we should use phones in class.
5 She ____________________ (not understand) what I'm saying.
6 What ____________________ you ____________________ (think) about?
7 ____________________ you ____________________ (read) anything interesting right now?
8 They ____________________ (not have) a very good day today.

UNIT 1 — expressing ability

Function

We can express general ability in the present with *can* or *am/is/are able to*. We can express general ability in the past with *could* or *was/were able to*. To express a particular ability, we can use phrases such as *manage* (+ infinitive) and *succeed in* (+ gerund).

Form

Present ability	Past ability
I can speak two languages. I can't speak three languages.	He could play the violin at the age of five. He couldn't play the violin at the age of three.
I'm able to remember people's faces easily. I'm not able to learn people's names easily.	He was able to play the French horn 10 years ago. He was not able to compose music 10 years ago.

A Choose the correct option.

1 People who **can** / **able to** speak two languages are often valued by employers.
2 When I was young, I **am** / **was** able to develop an ear for music.
3 They have succeeded **in learning** / **to learn** Portuguese.
4 She managed **in learning** / **to learn** the guitar without a teacher.

5 Can you **play** / **to play** the piano without looking at the piano keys?
6 He **has succeeded** / **was able to** learn the Korean alphabet in only two hours.
7 Benjamin is able **hear** / **to hear** a song once and remember all the words.
8 Not many people **succeed in** / **manage to** become professional musicians.

B Rewrite the sentences in a different way.

1 I couldn't swim until I was a teenager. *I wasn't able to swim until I was a teenager.*
2 He can name a hundred different kinds of fish. ______
3 Are you able to sing as well as your mother? ______
4 We weren't able to take private music lessons. ______
5 I can't explain the difference between a viola and a violin. ______
6 Could you speak English when you were young? ______

UNIT 2 — tag questions

Function

We use tag questions for two main purposes: to invite someone to agree with our opinion and to confirm information that we think is correct.

Form

Sentences with *be* form tags with *be*. Sentences with modals form tags with the modal. Sentences with other verbs form tags with forms of *do* or *have*. When the verb in the main part of the sentence is positive, the verb in the tag is negative. When the verb in the main part of the sentence is negative, the verb in the tag is positive.

Affirmative verbs	Negative verbs
Horses **are** intelligent, **aren't they**?	That dog **isn't** very smart, **is it**?
He **is feeding** the elephant, **isn't he**?	That horse **isn't** tame, **is it**?
You **love** animals, **don't you**?	Pigeons **don't use** tools, **do they**?
She **swam** with dolphins, **didn't she**?	The cat **didn't pass** the mirror test, **did it**?
They**'ve been** to a zoo before, **haven't they**?	He **hasn't ever** had a pet, **has he**?
Parrots **can** talk, **can't they**?	We **shouldn't do** tests on animals, **should we**?

A Match the sentence beginnings (1–8) to the sentence ends (a–h).

1 You don't like to visit zoos, ______
2 Dogs are very smart, ______
3 You can't train a cat to do tricks easily, ______
4 She volunteered at a dog rescue center, ______
5 You didn't have a pet as a child, ______
6 Chimpanzees can learn sign language, ______
7 He doesn't want to see the dolphin show, ______
8 Monkeys don't make good pets, ______

a did you?
b can you?
c does he?
d can't they?
e do you?
f didn't she?
g do they?
h aren't they?

B Complete the sentences with a tag question.

1 Dogs are more intelligent than cats, ______?
2 You don't need to feed snakes every day, ______?
3 A fish doesn't require as much care as a bird, ______?
4 Cats should not eat chocolate, ______?
5 You've worked with animals before, ______?
6 You care about animals as much as I do, ______?
7 It's not a good idea to feed fish more than once a day, ______?
8 We need to teach children not to harm animals, ______?

UNIT 2 — articles

Function

We use indefinite articles (*a*, *an*) before nouns to indicate the nouns are general. We use the definite article (*the*) before nouns to indicate they are specific. Sometimes we do not use any article at all.

Form

Use	Example
Use *a*/*an* with a singular countable noun when being general.	A veterinarian takes care of animals.
Use *a*/*an* when mentioning a singular countable noun for the first time. You can add an adjective between the article and the noun.	I heard there is a new veterinarian in town.
Use *the* with a singular countable noun when being specific.	The school counselor talked to us about careers.
Use *the* with a singular countable noun when referring to all members of a group in a general way.	The elephant is known for its intelligence, loyalty, and strength.
Use *the* with plural countable nouns when being specific.	The jobs that involved working with animals sound interesting.
Use *the* when there is only one of something.	Wolves sometimes seem to howl at the moon.
Use no article with plural countable nouns when talking generally.	Dolphins and whales are very intelligent.
Use no article with singular uncountable nouns when talking generally.	Stress can be an issue when working with animals.

A Choose the correct article. If no article is needed, choose X.

Have you ever thought about getting **1 a / the** job at **2 an / the** animal rescue shelter? **3 X / The** work can sometimes be hard, but it is **4 a / the** rewarding experience for **5 X / the** right person. Shelter managers often need to spend time raising funds in **6 X / the** community, so they depend on **7 X / the** volunteers to help out with animal care. The job pays as much in satisfaction as in **8 X / the** money.

B Complete the sentences with *a*, *an*, *the*, or *X* (no article).

1 We're thinking of getting ____________ pet, but we're not sure what kind.
2 My sister studies whales that migrate from ____________ Arctic Ocean.
3 I know several people who work as ____________ dog walkers.
4 Did anyone ever find ____________ dog that went missing in the neighborhood?
5 I don't think working as ____________ animal trainer is the right job for me.
6 Where can I get ____________ information on veterinary schools?

UNIT 3 — future time clauses (*after, as soon as, before, until, when*)

Function

We can use a time clause to talk about a possible future event. The time clause is introduced with a subordinating conjunction such as *after*, *as soon as*, *before*, *until*, or *when*. The time clause in the simple present tense can come before or after the main clause in the simple future tense. When the time clause comes first, add a comma after it.

Form

Main clause	Time clause
I will tell you my opinion I won't believe that story	after you tell me yours. until I check its source.

Time clause	Main clause
After you tell me your opinion, Until I check its source,	I will tell you mine. I won't believe that story.

A Complete the sentences with the simple present or simple future form of the verb in parentheses.

1 When I call you tomorrow, I ______________ (have) some good news.
2 The class will be quiet as soon as the teacher ______________ (come) in.
3 I ______________ (not be) able to finish this report until I get home.
4 After the students ______________ (finish) class, they will go out for a snack.
5 Don't worry. Sarah ______________ (finish) the presentation before she leaves the office.
6 The company ______________ (not hire) any new employees before the New Year.

B Combine the two sentences into one using the subordinating conjunction in parentheses. Be sure to use correct verb tenses in the clauses.

1 I (get) to work today. I (talk) to my boss about a raise. (after)

____

2 She (finish) this report. She (be) a lot happier! (when)

____

3 He (not provide) feedback on my paper. He (see) the final version. (until)

____

4 I (help) my colleague with her project. I (leave) the office today. (before)

____

5 I (purchase) a new computer. I (save) enough money. (as soon as)

____

6 You (need) help with your essay. I (be) happy to help you. (if)

____

UNIT 3 — present perfect progressive

Function

In some cases, we can use either the present perfect simple or the present perfect progressive tense with no change in meaning. In other cases, there is a difference in meaning or emphasis. We use the present perfect simple primarily to express that an action is completed or to emphasize its result. We use the present perfect progressive to emphasize the duration or continuous nature of an action. Stative verbs (*know*, *believe*, *understand*, etc.) are generally not used in the present perfect progressive.

Form

Present perfect simple (emphasizes completion or result of action)	**Present perfect progressive** (emphasizes duration or continuous nature of action)
I've worked here since 2017.	I've been working here since 2017.
Voice recognition software has improved.	Voice recognition software has been improving.
Humans have used machines for many years.	Humans have been using machines for many years.

Use	Example
Use the present perfect progressive for an action that began in the past and continues into the present.	Brian has been working on artificial intelligence for over 10 years.
Use the present perfect progressive to focus on an action that may or may not be completed.	Bethany and I have been working on our presentation.
Use the present perfect progressive to talk about an action that is temporary.	They have been working a lot of hours at the lab recently.

A Complete the sentences with the present perfect progressive form of the verb in parentheses.

1 I ______________________ (try) to understand this new software.
2 Lisa ______________________ (not come) to our science study group lately.
3 Scientists ______________________ (work) on AI technologies for many years.
4 Our math class ______________________ (get) harder and harder.
5 Gina ______________________ (study) really hard for the past month.
6 We ______________________ (not go) to the gym much lately.

B Unscramble and write questions using the present perfect progressive.

1 been / have / what / lately / you / doing

____

2 video games / been / have / they / playing

____

3 coming / recently / has / been / Aaron / to class

____

4 learning / have / been / why / they / how to / code

____

5 been / money / you / have / saving / for college

____

UNIT 4 — infinitives with *to*

Form and Function

Some words are followed by a *to* infinitive (*to* + verb).

Form and Use	Example
Use an infinitive to express a purpose to mean *in order to*.	I went to the bookstore (in order) to look for a book on public speaking.
Use an infinitive after some verbs (*agree*, *like*, *prefer*, *need*, *want*, etc.).	I don't really like to speak in a group that I don't know well.
Use an infinitive after some adjectives (*easy*, *happy*, *hard*, *good*, *ready*, etc.).	It's not easy to find good research material for some presentations.
Use an infinitive after some verbs (*warn*, *advise*, *persuade*, *tell*, etc.) and an object.	He persuaded me to use visual aids in my presentation.

A Choose the correct option.

1 Our teacher **agreed** / **told** us to watch the Steve Jobs documentary.
2 I didn't **agree** / **warn** to participate in the conference call today.
3 She would **prefer** / **say** to work alone on this week's project.
4 My roommate **persuaded** / **liked** me to go to the lecture.
5 Jason **went** / **ready** to check out a book from the library.
6 I would be **easy** / **happy** to help you with your presentation.

B Complete the sentences with the infinitive form of the verbs in the box.

apply be communicate copy find improve listen see

What separates a good leader from a great one? Look to history **1** ______________ the answer—Martin Luther King Jr., Mahatma Gandhi, Oprah Winfrey, Steve Jobs. It is easy **2** ______________ that communication was central to their success. They all used their own communication style **3** ______________ ideas. They used their gifts to persuade others **4** ______________. People who want **5** ______________ great communicators can do so. It's a skill anyone can learn **6** ______________ in various aspects of their lives. So if feel you are ready **7** ______________ your communication skills, be true to yourself. People who try **8** ______________ the successes of others are never successful.

UNIT 4 — separable and non-separable phrasal verbs

Function

A phrasal verb is a combination of a verb plus a particle (a small word like a preposition) that means something different from the verb and the particle. Phrasal verbs that take an object can be separable or inseparable. For separable phrasal verbs, if the object is a noun, it can go between the verb and the particle or after the particle. If the object is a pronoun, it can only go between the verb and the particle, but not after the particle. For non-separable phrasal verbs, a noun or pronoun can only go after the particle. Three-word phrasal verbs are non-separable.

Form

Separable phrasal verbs	Non-separable phrasal verbs
I need to clean up the house. I need to clean the house up. I need to clean it up. ~~I need to clean up it~~.	I ran into Jeff at the mall. I ran into him at the mall. ~~I ran Jeff into at the mall~~. ~~I ran him into at the mall~~.
Other examples: *fill out, throw away, pick up, turn off, put off, try on, turn down, ask out, call off, get across, make up*	**Other examples:** *take care of, call off, come across, count on, stick to, get rid of, keep up with, run out of, cut back on*

A Choose the correct sentence.

1 **a** You need to stick to your original plan. **b** You need to stick your original plan to.
2 **a** I really should cut down on sugar. **b** I really should cut down sugar on.
3 **a** Let me know if you come my notes across. **b** Let me know if you come across my notes.
4 **a** Can you help me clean this up? **b** Can you help me clean up this?
5 **a** If you like the jacket, try on it. **b** If you like the jacket, try it on.
6 **a** Let's put off this for another day. **b** Let's put this off for another day.
7 **a** I forgot to call back her again. **b** I forgot to call her back again.
8 **a** You know you can always count me on. **b** You know you can always count on me.

B Rewrite the sentences. Change the underlined noun to the pronoun in parentheses.

1 You can always count on <u>Maggie</u>. (her) ______________________________
2 I need you to fill in <u>this form</u> now. (it) ______________________________
3 Who takes care of <u>your children</u>? (them) ______________________________
4 Try to get across <u>your key points</u>. (them) ______________________________
5 Can you please turn down <u>the radio</u>? (it) ______________________________
6 It's hard to keep up with <u>Estefan</u>. (him) ______________________________
7 It's not too late to call off <u>the meeting</u>. (it) ______________________________
8 It's time to get rid of <u>your bad habits</u>. (them) ______________________________

UNIT 5 — review of conditionals

Function

Conditional sentences express the idea that an action in the main clause can only take place if a condition in the *if* clause is fulfilled. The word *unless* is also used in conditional clauses to express a negative condition.

- The zero conditional is used for situations that are real, and it is often used for general truths about the present. Both clauses are in the simple present tense.
- The first conditional is used for situations that are possible or likely in the future. The main clause is in the future tense, and the *if* clause is in the simple present tense.
- The second conditional is for unreal, hypothetical situations, or situations that are not true. The main clause is in the past tense, and the *if* clause uses *would* + *(not)* + the base form of the verb. If the verb is *be* in the main clause, *were* is used for both singular and plural objects.

Form

Zero conditional	First conditional	Second conditional
If water reaches 100 degrees, it boils. When it rains a lot in a short time, you get a flash flood. Plants die unless they get enough water.	A lot of crops will die if we don't get rain. If sea levels rise, a lot of people will need to move. If we don't do something, climate change will get worse.	If it weren't so rainy, I would go for a walk. Our oceans would be less polluted if we used less unrecyclable plastic. If we used greener energy, the world would be a better place.

A Choose *GT* (general truth), *PS* (possible situation), or *HS* (hypothetical situation) for each sentence.

1	If I had more time, I would volunteer at the aquarium.	GT	PS	HS
2	When the sun goes down, it gets dark.	GT	PS	HS
3	Unless it rains, we'll go to the beach tomorrow.	GT	PS	HS
4	You waste heat if you leave your windows open.	GT	PS	HS
5	We will have 10 members if you join our group.	GT	PS	HS
6	People would use less fuel if they traveled less.	GT	PS	HS

B Choose the correct form of the verb in parentheses.

1 If you ______________ (push) that button, it lights up.
2 If the winds get stronger, we ______________ (have) a hurricane.
3 What would you do if you ______________ (see) a tornado?
4 There ______________ (not be) any class tomorrow unless it stops snowing.
5 Ice melts when it ______________ (reach) a certain temperature.
6 The world ______________ (be) a better place if people cared more for each other.
7 The forest fire will be out of control unless the firefighters ______________ (get) there soon.
8 If it ______________ (snow) again this spring, I would be really surprised.

UNIT 5 — present and future hopes and wishes

Function

We can use the verbs *hope* and *wish* to talk about present and future hopes and wishes.

Form

Form and Use	Example
Use *hope* (+ subject) + simple present, present progressive, or *can* to express something that you want and expect to be true in the present.	I hope a lot of people are attending the march to save the environment today.
Use *hope* (+ subject) + simple present, *will*, or *can* to express something that you want and expect to happen in the future.	I hope our government can find a way to reduce the cost of a university education.
Use *wish* (+ subject) + *would* or *could* to express something that you would like to happen in the future, but that probably won't.	I wish more people would get involved in trying to solve our country's problems.
Use *wish* (+ subject) + simple past to express something that you would like to be true in the present, but that isn't now.	I wish people spent less money on unnecessary electronics.

A Unscramble and write the sentences.

1 I / like / you / environmental poster / my / hope ______
2 fossil fuels / used / they / she / wishes / fewer ______
3 stop / will / he / hopes / global warming ______
4 help / we / our campaign / wish / you / could / with ______
5 money / some / can / you / I / donate / hope ______
6 our ideas / wish / reject / I / you / wouldn't ______

B Choose the correct option.

1 I hope I **get** / **would get** a job with a green company.
2 I wish people **will care** / **would care** more about our environment.
3 Do ever wish you **can change** / **could change** just one law?
4 I hope businesses **are listening** / **would listen** to the eco-needs of their customers.
5 I wish I **major** / **had majored** in environmental science.
6 She hopes other students **can help** / **could help** in her letter-writing campaign.
7 He wishes more people **appreciate** / **would appreciate** the dangers facing our environment.
8 Our teacher hopes her students **will participate** / **would participate** in the Earth Day celebrations.

UNIT 6 — past perfect

Function

We use the past perfect to show that one past action happened before another action in the past. The past perfect is formed with *had* + past participle.

Form

Affirmative statements	Negative statements
I had read all my email by the time I ate breakfast. All of Marta's friends had gotten cell phones before she did. They knew the city well, as they had visited it several times previously.	I failed the history exam because I hadn't studied very hard. Before Ian went to Tokyo, he had never seen so many people. They didn't get into the theater because they hadn't booked a ticket in advance.

A Choose the action (a or b) that happened first.

1 **a** Karl had owned his baseball card collection for 30 years, **b** so he felt bad about selling it.
2 **a** People had had cell phones for years by the time **b** the iPhone hit the market.
3 **a** Steve didn't understand the talk because **b** he hadn't read the speaker's book.
4 **a** When I got to the train station this morning, **b** the train had already left.
5 **a** Many people had attempted to fly before **b** the Wright Brothers made their first successful flight.

B Complete the sentences with the correct form of the verb in parentheses. Use one simple past verb and one past perfect verb in each sentence.

1 I ______________ (know) how to use the new software because I ______________(try) it before.
2 Luckily, I ______________ (save) my document before my computer ______________ (crash).
3 We ______________ (not be) to Los Angeles before, so we ______________ (get) lost right away.
4 The plane ______________ (leave) by the time I ______________ (get) to the airport.
5 Cars ______________ (be) expensive before the assembly line ______________ (make) them affordable.

UNIT 6 — defining relative clauses

Function

A defining relative clause usually comes immediately after the noun or noun phrase it describes. It gives information that defines or identifies the person, thing, time, or place.

Form

Use	Example
Use *that* to refer to a thing.	A car that drives itself sounds like an amazing idea.
Use *who* to refer to a person.	The employee who designs new software is over there.
Use *where* to refer to a place.	I live in a large city where there is a lot of innovation.
Use *when* to refer to a time.	That was a time when things were much simpler.

A Complete the sentences with *that*, *who*, *where*, or *when*.

1 This camera ______________ is on my smartphone is better than some expensive cameras.
2 Can you think back to a time ______________ you weren't connected 24/7?
3 That arcade is the place ______________ I first learned how to play video games.
4 Please give me the name of the person ______________ sold you this 3-D printer.
5 The late 20th century was a time ______________ there were great innovations in communications.
6 Do you know the name of the person ______________ first climbed Mount Everest?
7 I want a cell phone ______________ fits neatly into my front shirt pocket.
8 The usual place ______________ my friend and I hang out is the mall.

B Find and correct one error in each sentence.

1 This is the place when everyone gets their SIM cards. ______________
2 This is the card where will get you a 30% discount. ______________
3 I know a guy builds websites for free. ______________
4 Think of an everyday product who you can't live without. ______________
5 She lived at a time who people made their own clothes. ______________
6 Do you know the woman standing by the door is? ______________

Unit 1

Track 2

Welcome to today's lecture in our Introduction to Psychology course. Over the last few lectures, we looked at the development of the brain, and this week I want to talk about abilities. Now, we all have various abilities, but I want to talk about two that some people have and others don't. These are perfect pitch and advanced language learning.

To begin with, people with perfect pitch can hear a musical note and tell you exactly what it is. According to the magazine *Psychology Today*, only 1 in 10,000 people has this ability. Mariah Carey has perfect pitch, and so did Mozart. As you probably know, Mozart could play the violin and the keyboard at the age of five. And he managed to write his first symphony at the age of eight. He wrote amazing music for the whole of his short life. He died of illness at the age of 35, but his music still brings happiness to people today. Interestingly, more people have perfect pitch in Asia. There is a possibility that this is because some languages in Asia use different tones.

Moving on to language learning, we all have the ability to learn a language. In fact, we all learn at least one language, our own, to a high level. And many of us have succeeded in learning one or two foreign languages. However, some people are able to learn languages with incredible speed. For example, Daniel Tammet, a writer from England, can speak 10 languages. For a TV program, he went to Iceland and gave himself one week to learn Icelandic. Amazingly, after a week, he could speak the language well enough to be interviewed on national TV. That was a real achievement.

Now I'd like to explore what is happening in the brains of people with these amazing abilities …

Track 3

1 able ability
2 available availability

Track 4

Host: Welcome to The Dave Goldstein Podcast. I'm your host, Dave Goldstein. On today's show, we're talking about amazing stories of survival. And with me is journalist and writer Ellen Delgado. Ellen, you've just written a book on people who have survived tough situations. Tell us about it.

Ellen: Thanks for having me on the show, Dave. Yes, while I was writing my book, I learned about some amazing survival stories.

Host: And do you have a favorite story?

Ellen: Yes. I think the person I respect the most was a very brave woman called Juliane Koepcke , who was born in Lima, Peru. When she was 17, in 1971, she was traveling by plane over the Amazonian rain forest when lightning hit the plane. The plane broke up at a height of 3.2 kilometers, and Juliane fell all that way in her seat!

Host: But she survived?

Ellen: Yes. People think that the seat she was in saved her when she crashed into the trees. When she woke up the following morning, she was alone in the rainforest, a long way from other people. The only food she had was a bag of candy. Luckily, Juliane was a calm, independent person. She found a stream and followed it. That was a good piece of logical thinking. After nine days, she found a boat and a small hut. She waited there, and the next day she was discovered by some men, who gave her food and then took her back to civilization.

Host: That's amazing. And what happened to her after that?

Ellen: She became a scientist and went back to the rain forests of Peru. She studied bats there. Later, she moved to Germany, and in 2011 wrote her autobiography, called When I Fell from the Sky, all about her amazing story of survival. If you're curious, you can read her story in her own words there.

Host: That's a great story of survival. We'll be back with more from Ellen after this break.

Unit 2

Track 02

Good morning, everyone, and thank you very much to the college for inviting me here today to speak to all of you. My name's Nancy Rubin, and I'm a career advisor. I'm here to talk about careers with animals and help you look at your options. I think everyone will be familiar with some professions, such as zookeepers and veterinarians, but there are many others, too. It's important to know what qualities employers are looking for, what exams you need to pass, and what experience is required. So, let's start by looking at a familiar career, and then one that's a bit more unusual!

Track 3

The first career I'd like to mention is marine biologist. Now, of course, *marine* refers to the sea, so a marine biologist is someone who studies animals that live in the sea. That can be anything from whales to tiny creatures called plankton. Marine biology is a large field and it covers many different careers. Many marine biologists are research scientists. They might spend the summer months doing research and the winter months teaching at a university. Marine biologists should be prepared for harsh conditions. They don't always work with dolphins in warm waters! If you choose this career path, you'll need a degree in biology or marine biology, and you'll probably then have to go to graduate school and possibly get a doctoral degree.

The second career I'd like to mention is a bit more unusual. It's a snake milker!

Now, you know that we milk cows, and sometimes sheep and goats, but how do you milk a snake? Snakes don't have milk. They have venom, the poison they use to kill the animals they eat. A snake milker takes venom from a snake. Why? The venom is very useful. First of all, it's used to make antivenom, which we need when a snake bites someone. The venom also has other medical uses. If you choose *this* career, you will need a degree in biology, chemistry, or biochemistry. And you will also need a lot of practical training!

Now let's look at another job related to animals—a zoologist …

Track 4

I have to take my dog to the vet.

My dog has to stay in the animal hospital.

Track 5

Thank you and hello everyone! Welcome to our open day here at Rashford Zoo. It's great to have the chance to speak to you about the work we do at the zoo. When you visit a zoo, you see animals in many different types of places. We try to provide an environment for each animal that is similar to where they live in the wild. That isn't always possible. We can't provide miles of ice and snow for the penguins, for example, but we try to get as close as we can. We want you, the visitor, to see the animals' natural behavior.

We also want to educate people about the dangers some animals face in the wild. We have posters around the zoo with information on them. Zookeepers also talk to members of the public about the threats to animals' habitats and what we can do about them. We have a responsibility to make sure that everyone knows the effects we humans have on nature.

Away from the public, we do a lot of work to help animals. Together with other zoos, we have breeding programs. When a species is endangered in the wild, we make sure there are enough animals in zoos to keep the species going. In some cases, for example wolves and pandas, we take animals from zoos and release them into the wild. That increases the numbers and helps the species to recover.

Now, if you'll all follow me, we'll go and see some of our zookeepers in action.

Unit 3

Track 2

Host: Hi, and welcome back to *Our World Today*. It's time once again for our weekly call-in. It seems that machines that can think, in other words, artificial intelligence, are becoming more common. Today's question is: What do you think of artificial intelligence? We've got Julia on line 1. Hi, Julia. What would you like to say?

Julia: I think there's no such thing as artificial intelligence. Scientists have been researching it since the 1950s. In that time, they've created machines that can play games like chess very well, but the machines aren't really thinking. They're just following rules. Only people can really think. Machines will never have the thinking power of a human. Humans have been thinking and solving problems for 200,000 years, and we've gotten very good at it!

Host: Thanks for that thought, Julia. And we've got Rafael on line 2. What's your opinion, Rafael?

Rafael: I disagree with the last caller. I think we already use artificial intelligence in different ways. Did you know that a commercial pilot only controls a plane for about seven minutes during a flight? The rest of the time it's controlled by the autopilot because humans get tired and bored and make mistakes. And driverless cars will all rely on AI to avoid accidents, and they'll probably be better at it than people. Some people think that it's only really AI if robots can fully communicate with us, but it isn't like that.

Host: Interesting points, Rafael. Thank you. Megan now on line 3.

Megan: Hello. I've been thinking about AI a lot recently, and I think there's something everyone has forgotten. Who is going to be in control of the machines in the future? I mean, when machines can think, will they be a danger to us? We create computer systems to control everything, and now some are really complicated. No human understands exactly what they are doing. I think that's a dangerous situation.

Host: Hmm … something to think about there. Thanks, Megan. Finally, Victor on line 4.

Victor: I'm worried about the effect on people's working lives. According to researchers at Oxford University, 47% of jobs in the US might be done by machines in the future. It'll have an effect on people who work in services: office workers, truck drivers and taxi drivers, and even people like receptionists and shop assistants. We won't need to employ people when AI becomes powerful enough. And what are we going to do then?

Host: Good question, Victor. Thanks to everyone for your views on this subject …

Host: … some really interesting points. Next week we will be talking about …

Track 3

1 Some people **say** that AI is a danger.
2 My mom **says** that she'll never lose her job to a robot.
3 My dad **said** the same thing and then lost his job!

Track 4

Hello, everyone! It's great to be here to talk to you today about being creative. Now, I know that we all have times when it's hard to be creative. You're trying to solve a problem and you just don't have any ideas. It's easy to give up and think that you aren't a creative person. Or make up excuses and say that it was too hard, or you didn't have enough time. I'm here today to tell you that we can all be creative if we use the right methods. I've come up with a few easy ways to be more creative that we can all rely on.

One thing you can do is make sure you have the knowledge you need. Become an expert. Look up information online and learn about an area. Creative people get ideas by understanding other people's ideas. The more you know, the more your ideas grow.

Another thing you can do is take up a sport or hobby. When you do that, you put yourself in the position of being a beginner. When you get good at a sport, it's easy to stop learning and to think you know everything about it. Trying a new sport helps you remember what it's like not to know all the answers.

Track 5

Here are a few very simple exercises that people have been using for a long time to help them be more creative. The first is a way of coming up with lots of ideas. You take an ordinary object, such as a spoon or a paper clip, and you try to think of as many different uses for it as you can in three minutes. For example, a paper clip could be used to open a lock, or to eat cheese, or to tie your hair back!

For the second method, you need to write two lists of very different objects. It doesn't matter what they are, but you need to make them all different. Then you choose an object from the first list and an object from the second list. You have to find ways in which the objects are the same. For example, you might have an elephant and a flower. How could they be the same? Well, maybe you can see both at a zoo, or maybe an elephant's ears are like a flower's petals! Or maybe they both need water every day!

The third exercise uses famous people. Let's say you're coming up with ideas to solve a problem. You might ask: "What would the president do?" Or "What would Mickey Mouse do?" Or "What would my favorite singer do?" The answers to these questions might be silly, but they also might tell you something about the problem.

Another way to encourage creativity is to …

Unit 4

Track 2

Host: Hello, and welcome to the *Career Report*. This week's guest is Jayden Ross. Jayden's a psychologist who studies nonverbal communication. Jayden, welcome to the podcast.

Jayden: Good to be here.

Host: Now, we all know that communication skills are very important. What can you tell us about communication?

Jayden: There are three parts to it, really. The first is the things we *say*, the actual *words* we use. Researchers believe that words are only 7% of what we communicate.

Host: Is that all? That's amazing.

Jayden: Yes, it's much less than most people think. Then there's the *way* we speak. That's around 38% of what we communicate.

Host: Okay. I'm guessing that includes tone of voice, speed, volume, things like that.

Jayden: That's right. And the rest, around 55%, is body language, all the things we do with our body when we are talking or when we are listening to someone else.

Track 3

Host: So, tell us about the way we speak.

Jayden: Your tone of voice plays a big part in communication. We all know that if you ask someone how they are, the *way* they say "I'm fine" can communicate a lot. It can communicate that the person really *is* fine, or it can communicate that the person *isn't* fine and wants you to ask how they really are! That's one reason why communicating by email or text message can create problems. There's no tone of voice, so it's easy to misunderstand someone's meaning.

Host: I see. And what about body language?

Jayden: First of all, there's personal space. There's usually a distance between you and the person you are talking to. And it changes in different cultures. Your listeners can look this up on the internet. People in Argentina, for example, want a distance of about 76 centimeters when they are talking to strangers. In Mexico, it's a meter, and in Romania, it's 1.4 meters.

Host: Interesting! What else?

Jayden: The expression on your face says a lot, and so does the position of your arms and hands. Open arms generally mean that you are open to another person's opinion, and arms across your body usually mean you don't want to listen. Touch is also important in some cultures.

Host: Okay, so is there any general advice you can give our listeners about understanding body language?

Jayden: Don't rely on just a person's words or their body language. Look at them both together. Check when a person's words and body language *aren't* saying the same thing. If a person is saying something friendly but their body is saying the opposite, that's when you need to be careful!

Host: Jayden Ross, thanks for joining us today.

Track 4

We live in an age where communication is global and fast. You can contact anyone at any time through email, text message, or instant messaging. However, it wasn't always that way, and there are clear technological steps that have led us to where we are today.

These days, we all use email, and we send over 280 billion emails a day! Email has come a long way since it was invented in 1971. That was when a computer engineer named Ray Tomlinson sent the first email message—to himself! That was just a couple of years before the first cell phone appeared. Today, something like 67% of the world's population owns and uses a cell phone.

Many people use cell phones to send text messages, or SMS messages. SMS means "short message service," and the first SMS was sent in December 1992—it said "Merry Christmas." Today, we send text messages every day. Many people include emojis in their messages. Emojis were invented in 1999 by a Japanese designer, Shigetaka Kurita. He created 176 images, and today there are over 2,800 emojis. One of the most popular ones is the "face with tears of laughter."

The next big step in communication was the first mass-marketed smartphone, the iPhone. Apple brought it out in 2007. Today over 2 million apps are available for the iPhone. One of the most popular apps is WhatsApp, used for instant messaging. It first appeared in 2009, and today people send 55 billion messages a day through the service. A couple of years later, in 2011, a service began that allowed users to send pictures that disappear. Of course, this is Snapchat, and today 188 million people use it to communicate.

Now let's think about how different types of people use different means of communication.

Track 5

Lisa:

Go to www.macmillan.com

My email is lisa_jackson3@emailtoday.org

Under the picture, it says #selfie and #mybestlook

My email is carrie-smith@fly.org

Unit 5

Track 2

1 reduce pollution
2 provide recycling
3 create laws
4 pay for plastic bags
5 require less packaging
6 use clean energy

Track 3

Host: Good afternoon. You're listening to KT Radio, and we're on the street today talking to young people about environmental issues. It's a little noisy here, so I hope you can hear me! Excuse me. What's your name, and what do you think is the biggest environmental problem today?

Eric: Uh, hi. I'm Eric Tyler. To me, the most important environmental issue is air pollution. Air pollution is caused by burning fossil fuels, and that causes global warming. If global warming continues, our planet will die. I wish fossil fuels didn't exist! We should have lower taxes for companies that use clean energy.

Host: Thanks, Eric. And how about you? Can you give me your name and tell us what you think?

Susan: Sure. My name is Susan Dyson. I think water pollution is the biggest problem. Millions of people in the world do not have clean water to drink. I wish every country had stronger laws against water pollution.

Host: Thank you, Susan. And what do you think? Sorry, what's your name?

Ali: I'm Ali Rahman. In my opinion, trash is the worst environmental problem. We are throwing away tons of trash, especially plastic. I wish we could completely stop using plastic bags and packages. I hope all cities will provide free recycling soon.

Host: Thanks, Ali. And … hi. What's your name?

Anh: My name is Anh Dao. I wish my government would make fishing companies reduce certain types of fishing. Fishing is very important for our economy, and if the fish populations were destroyed, it would be terrible for my country. I hope our generation makes a lot of changes to help save the planet!

Host: Thank you all, and Anh, that's a very good point. We're all young, and it's up to us. I hope our generation is taking environmental problems seriously, and I hope we will be more responsible.

Track 4

Professor: Good afternoon, everyone. Now, as we discussed yesterday, there are many excellent government projects happening in countries around the world that aim to create solutions to environmental problems. There are also many new products invented by small or large businesses to address these problems. For example, several small companies here in the US are making plant pots from old automobile tires. The pots are attractive, and the tires don't go into the trash! So, I asked you to do some research. What did you find out?

Joe: I found a really interesting project that's kind of weird but cool. A company in Indonesia called Paper Flops is making flip-flops out of recycled paper, coconut shells, palm tree roots, and natural rubber. Also, they teach homeless children and disabled people to make the sandals, so they're helping people as well as the environment!

Professor: Sounds great! Molly, what did you find?

Molly: Well, they're doing a lot of things to make Singapore green—planting a lot of trees and creating parks, for example, but my favorite thing is the giant structures called super trees. The trees are made of steel, but they have thousands of climbing plants and flowers. The trees also generate solar power and collect rainwater, so they help the environment in several ways. I hope other cities will put in super trees! How about you, Jorge?

Jorge: Wow … bizarre! I'd love to see them. OK. I'm from Chile, so I wanted to research environmental solutions in Latin America. I found a really interesting project in Mexico. A company called Eco Domum is making houses from recycled plastic. They use the plastic to make the walls and roof of the buildings. I think it's a great idea. Another project is producing water in very dry areas in Chile and Peru. They use giant nets to catch drops of water from fog. They hope that in the future, they can produce enough water for all of the people in the desert areas.

Professor: Very interesting. And, finally, Asami, what can you tell us?

Asami: One of the biggest problems in the world is plastic trash, and in Kenya, a company called Eco Dawati is recycling plastic to make desks for schools. A lot of schools have never had desks, so it's great for the kids. It uses plastic trash in a practical way to help people. The next two things are kind of similar. The first one is living walls—walls that have plants growing on them. They look pretty, and they produce oxygen. They're using these living walls in many places, including England. The other one is green roofs. I was interested in this one because they're doing it in my country, Japan. When I go home, I hope I can live in a building with a green roof!

Professor: You've all done a great job, and it's good to remember that many countries around the world are doing things to help the environment. If governments and companies in every country did just a few of these things, our planet would be a lot cleaner and healthier. Sometimes wild ideas are the best ones!

Unit 6

Track 2

Interviewer: Good evening everyone. I'm Melissa Warren and for today's show, I'm on a street where lots of young people hang out on Saturday evenings. I'm going to ask some people their opinions about inventions from the first two decades of the 21st century, and which inventions they think will be considered the most historic in the future.
Excuse me, sir. I'm from Channel 9 TV, and I'm asking people to give their opinions about 21st-century inventions. Are there any that you think will have historic importance?

Man 1: Uh, yeah, maybe 3-D printers. Those could have historic importance. Actually, I'm pretty worried about several of the recent inventions, but to me, the invention that is the most worrying so far is the 3-D printer. If there's a time when people can make most of their own products, it will be very bad for business.

Interviewer: That's an interesting point, thank you. What about you, ma'am? In your opinion, are there any historic 21st-century inventions so far?

Woman 1: Well, there are a lot of amazing new inventions. I'm a photographer, and I think one of the most exciting inventions is a camera that can take 360-degree pictures. I'm really excited because these cameras are totally changing professional photography. I don't know if it's a historic invention, but it's important in my career.

Interviewer: I see, thank you for that. Excuse me, sir, which 21st-century inventions do you think are the most interesting or exciting?

Man 2: Well, I'm really amused by some of the things that have been invented recently. Apparently, somebody has invented a little hammock for feet, and I think that's really funny. There are some inventors who are creating some pretty amusing things!

Interviewer: Yes, I guess some inventions are more amusing than useful. They probably won't have historic importance. Excuse me, ma'am, can I ask your opinion about 21st-century inventions?

Woman 2: Sure. Driverless cars are amazing, but are those cars going to be safe in big cities, where there is a lot of traffic? I'm worried about that. I guess there are a lot of people who want to read or check their text messages and let their car drive, but not me! Anyway, I think driverless cars will have a huge effect on transportation.

Interviewer: Yes, I totally agree that driverless cars are a historic invention. I think there are some people who are worried about driverless cars, but I'm sure the technology will improve a lot before there are many of them on the streets.

Track 3

Today's subject on *Game Changers* is one of the most famous doctors in history. Before 1967, there had been transplants of several different human organs, but there had been no successful heart transplants. On December 3, 1967, South African heart surgeon *Christiaan Barnard* changed that forever.

Christiaan Barnard was born in South Africa in 1922, and he grew up in a poor family. Dr. Barnard got his medical degree at the University of Cape Town in South Africa and later studied cardiac surgery at the University of Minnesota in the US. Before he became a cardiac surgeon, Dr. Barnard had worked in medicine for several years, and he had found a cure for a fatal kidney defect.

Dr. Barnard was a very capable heart surgeon for 10 years before he attempted the first transplant. He introduced open-heart surgery to South Africa. Before he transplanted the first human heart, Dr. Barnard had practiced the operation on dogs, so he had had some experience with the procedure. In 1967, he felt that he was ready to do a human heart transplant, and he found a 54-year-old man with serious heart disease. The man's situation was hopeless, and he agreed to try a transplant. Dr. Barnard found a heart donor, and the operation was done. The transplant was successful, but the man died of pneumonia 18 days after the operation. Dr. Barnard went on to perform more heart transplants, and several of his patients lived for years after their transplants.

Today, over 7,000 heart transplants are performed every year, and deaths from heart disease are often preventable. The world is thankful to Dr. Christiaan Barnard for his wonderful contribution to heart patients everywhere. Before Dr. Barnard's incredible achievement, most people had not imagined that a heart transplant would ever be possible.

Track 4

hopeful	thankful	preventable
capable	successful	incredible

Macmillan Education
4 Crinan Street
London N1 9XW
A division of Macmillan Education Limited

Companies and representatives throughout the world

Speak Your Mind Level 3A Student's Book
ISBN 978-1-380-03142-6
Speak Your Mind Level 3A Student's Book + access to Student's App and Digital Workbook ISBN 978-1-380-03140-2
Speak Your Mind Level 3A Student's Book + access to Student's App
ISBN 978-1-380-03139-6

Written by Mickey Rogers, Joanne Taylore-Knowles, and Steve Taylore-Knowles

The authors have asserted their right to be identified as the authors of this work in accordance with the Copyright, Designs, and Patents Act 1988.

First published 2020

Designed by QBS Learning
Illustrated by QBS Learning pp. 13, 19, 41.
Cover design by therestless.co.uk
Cover adaptation by Roberto Martínez
Cover photographs by **Getty Images**/Chatuporn Sornlampoo/EyeEm (background); **Shutterstock**/Aaron Amat (lower body), Shutterstock/REALDEE (window), Shutterstock/ShotPrime Studio (upper body-blazer), Shutterstock/szefei (upper body).
Picture research by Fernanda Rocha/Ikonia LLC

Authors' acknowledgements
Mickey, Jo and Steve would like to thank everyone at Macmillan Education and RedNova Learning who have made this project possible and who have gone the extra mile (literally!) to meet up, work together, and throw around a million ideas, some of which even made their way into the books! Jo and Steve would also like to thank Scout for her patience and understanding and for letting her parents get on with it when they needed to!

The publishers would like to thank all the teachers that piloted and reviewed the series.

The authors and publishers would like to thank the following for permission to reproduce their photographs:
Alamy Stock Photo/Peter Casolino p. 20(dog handler), Alamy Stock Photo/Chronicle p. 58(cbr), Alamy Stock Photo/GL Archive p. 62(d), Alamy Stock Photo/Thierry GRUN p. 20(wildlife photographer), Alamy Stock Photo/imageBROKER p. 20(zookeeper), Alamy Stock Photo/Images by Itani p. 52(a), Alamy Stock Photo/Bulat Silvia p. 45(b), Alamy Stock Photo/Terry Whittaker Wildlife p. 20(zoologist), Alamy Stock Photo/Arman Zhenikeyev p. 20(horse trainer); Getty Images/AFP/Stringer p. 52(b), Getty Images/AzmanJaka p. 22(cr), Getty Images/ullstein bild/Contributor pp. 12, 62(b), Getty Images/Boston Globe/Contributor p. 8, Getty Images/Caiaimage/Paul Bradbury p. 58(ctr), Getty Images/Christian Ender/Contributor p. 6, Getty Images/filadendron p. 29, Getty Images/Maciej Frolow p. 60(f), Getty Images/Jure Gasparic/EyeEm p. 60(d), Getty Images/GK Hart/Vikki Hart p. 20(vet/veterinarian), Getty Images/Heritage Images/Contributor p. 10(l), Getty Images/Image by cuppyuppycake p. 17, Getty Images/JackF p. 22(j), Getty Images/Thanagon Karaket/EyeEm p. 60(b-notebook), Getty Images/Clodagh Kilcoyne/Contributor p. 62(a), Getty Images/Keith Ladzinski p. 7, Getty Images/Mikolette p. 39, Getty Images/Tara Moore pp. 28, Getty Images/Richard Newstead p. 50, Getty Images/Dennis O'Clair p. 37, Getty Images/Pekic p. 25, Getty Images/PeopleImages pp. 31, Getty Images/AndreyPopov p. 60(a), Getty Images/Mondadori Portfolio/Contributor p. 62(c), Getty Images/Roberto Ricciuti/Contributor p. 10(r), Getty Images/Christina Sarmiento/EyeEm p. 24, Getty Images/sbayram p. 22(c), Getty Images/serts p. 42(tr), Getty Images/John S Lander/Contributor p. 52(g), Getty Images/Sovfoto/Contributor p. 63, Getty Images/Ibrahim Suha Derbent p. 22(d), Getty Images/Alexander Spatari p. 52(h), Getty Images/Chase Swift p. 21, Getty Images/talevr p. 60(e), Getty Images/Rainer von Brandis p. 20(marine biologist), Getty Images/Klaus Vedfelt p. 40, Getty Images/vusta p. 22(e), Getty Images/Westend61 pp. 23, 26, 128, Getty Images/Wilfred Y Wong p. 52(d), Getty Images/10'000 Hours p. 45(m); Shutterstock/Africa Studio p. 15(7), Shutterstock/Edgar Airborne p. 14(b), Shutterstock/Alexxndr p. 137, Shutterstock/Aaron Amat p. 44, Shutterstock/Papa Annur p. 52(f), Shutterstock/ArchMan p. 22(g), Shutterstock/baranq p. 138, Shutterstock/Gyorgy Barna p. 46, Shutterstock/Rich Carey p22(f), Shutterstock/Steve Cukrov p. 52(e), Shutterstock/Iakov Filimonov p. 20(breeder), Shutterstock/flower travelin' man pp. 42(1-7), 43(emojis), Shutterstock/Georgejmclittle p. 141, Shutterstock/HomeStudio p. 15(3), Shutterstock/ImageFlow p. 60(c-background), Shutterstock/Eric Isselee pp. 22(a, i), Shutterstock/Alexsander Iusupov p. 60(b-background), Shutterstock/AlenKadr p. 131, Shutterstock/Anan Kaewkhammul p. 22(h), Shutterstock/KENG MERRY Paper Art pp. 54-55(b), Shutterstock/Klepach p. 54(cl), Shutterstock/plew koonyosying p. 52(c), Shutterstock/Jacob Lund p. 32(cr), Shutterstock/marylooo p. 15(4), Shutterstock/Mega Pixel pp. 36, 129, Shutterstock/Microgen p. 132, Shutterstock/Phonlamai Photo p. 30, Shutterstock/photokirov p. 15(8), Shutterstock/pogonici p. 16, Shutterstock/Mike Price p. 22(b), Shutterstock/Rawpixel.com p. 45(t), Shutterstock/restyler p. 15(1), Shutterstock/Sensay p. 57, Shutterstock/Siberian Photographer p. 127, Shutterstock/SSokolov p. 47, Shutterstock/Anton Starikov p. 15(5), Shutterstock/StockLite p. 38, Shutterstock/Thawornnurak p. 42(tl), Shutterstock/Alex Tuzhikov p. 60(c-hammock9), Shutterstock/vectorfusionart p.34, Shutterstock/Praiwan Wasanruk p. 32(br), Shutterstock/Waj p. 14(t), Shutterstock/wavebreakmedia p. 56, Shutterstock/White Space Ukraine p. 15(2), Shutterstock/Yellowj p. 60(b-shower), Shutterstock/Yeti studio p. 15(6), 123RF/kampwit p. 20(cr), 123RF/sellphoto1 p. 18.

Additional Sources:
p. 24, "Abandoned Dogs Roam Detroit in Packs as Humans Dwindle" by Chris Christoff, August 21, 2013, Bloomberg website. p. 28, "Measuring Consumer Information" by Roger Bohn and James E. Short, 2012, *International Journal of Communication*, Vol. 6, pp. 980–1000. p. 40, "Is Nonverbal Communication a Numbers Game?" by Jeff Thompson, September 30, 2011, *Psychology Today* website referencing Mehrabian, A. (1972). *Nonverbal Communication*. New Brunswick: Aldine Transaction. p. 40, "What 'Personal Space' Looks Like around the World" by Amanda Erickson, April 24, 2017, *The Washington Post* website. p. 42, "The Number of Emails Sent per Day in 2019 (and 20+ Other Email Facts)" by Henry Tschabitscher, January 3, 2019, *Lifewire* website. p. 42, "Number of Mobile Phone Users Worldwide from 2015 to 2020" by Statista, November 2016, Statista website. p. 42, Data from Appfigures, Appfigures website, 2018. p. 42, Data from WhatsApp, WhatsApp Blog website, 2018. p. 42, "Number of Daily Active Snapchat Users from 1st Quarter 2014 to 3rd Quarter 2018" by Statista, October 2018, Statista website. p. 46, "Digital Advertising to Surpass Print and TV for the First Time, Report Says" by Hamza Shaban, February 20, 2019, *The Washington Post* website. p. 46, Internet World Stats website, May 9, 2019. p. 48, "IPCC Press Release #2018/24/PR" by Intergovernmental Panel on Climate Change, October 8, 2018, IPCC website.

Printed and bound in Mexico
by Compañía Editorial Ultra, S.A. de C.V.

2021 2020
12 11 10 09